MAGAZINE

delicious.

FRUGAL FEASTS

HarperCollins*Publishers*
77–85 Fulham Palace Road,
Hammersmith, London W6 8JB
www.harpercollins.co.uk

First published by HarperCollins*Publishers* 2009

10 9 8 7 6 5 4 3 2

A catalogue record of this book is available from the British Library

ISBN-13   978-0-00-732837-6

Printed and bound in China by South China Printing Co., Ltd

delicious. MAGAZINE
FRUGAL FEASTS

Edited by Mitzie Wilson

Magazine Editor
Matthew Drennan

HarperCollins*Publishers*

contents

introduction

When you train to be a chef as I did, you learn many things about food in a busy restaurant kitchen, not least the importance of cost. My obsession with not wasting food or money didn't come from my parents or school teachers, no, that honour goes to the big sweaty chef standing over me watching what I did with every scrap of food.

The cost of food is something that affects all of us and that has even more resonance today. Where watching the pennies is concerned, what most people want are reassuring recipes that they know will not break the bank. At **delicious.** magazine we are continuously conscious of this.

In this book we have put together a collection of our recipes that we think will be timeless where taste and value is concerned and that you can reach for when feeding the family. The recipes are mainly founded on everyday low-cost ingredients, using up your storecupboard staples including spices and dried herbs and putting half-used jars of this and that to good use (particularly in the dessert section).

And don't think that because the recipes are frugal or budget you won't find some gems for entertaining friends and family. Believe me, they'll never know.

At **delicious.** magazine all the recipes are tested in our kitchen and we are satisfied that they will read, cook and taste to the highest standards, every time.

Matthew Drennan
delicious. Magazine Editor

Conversion tables

All the recipes in this book list only metric measurements (also used by Australian cooks). The conversions listed here are approximate for imperial measurements (also used by American cooks).

Oven temperatures

°C	Fan°C	°F	Gas	Description
110	90	225	¼	Very cool
120	100	250	½	Very cool
140	120	275	1	Cool
150	130	300	2	Cool
160	140	325	3	Warm
180	160	350	4	Moderate
190	170	375	5	Moderately hot
200	180	400	6	Fairly hot
220	200	425	7	Hot
230	210	450	8	Very hot
240	220	475	9	Very hot

Weights for dry ingredients

Metric	Imperial	Metric	Imperial
7g	¼oz	425g	15oz
15g	½oz	450g	1lb
20g	¾oz	500g	1lb 2oz
25g	1oz	550g	1¼lb
40g	1½oz	600g	1lb 5oz
50g	2oz	650g	1lb 7oz
60g	2½oz	675g	1½lb
75g	3oz	700g	1lb 9oz
100g	3½oz	750g	1lb 11oz
125g	4oz	800g	1¾lb
140g	4½oz	900g	2lb
150g	5oz	1kg	2¼lb
165g	5½oz	1.1kg	2½lb
175g	6oz	1.25kg	2¾lb
200g	7oz	1.35kg	3lb
225g	8oz	1.5kg	3lb 6oz
250g	9oz	1.8kg	4lb
275g	10oz	2kg	4½lb
300g	11oz	2.25kg	5lb
350g	12oz	2.5kg	5½lb
375g	13oz	2.75kg	6lb
400g	14oz	3kg	6¾lb

Liquid measures

Metric	imperial	Aus	US
25ml	1fl oz		
50ml	2fl oz	¼ cup	¼ cup
75ml	3fl oz		
100ml	3½fl oz		
120ml	4fl oz	½ cup	½ cup
150ml	5fl oz		
175ml	6 fl oz	¾ cup	¾ cup
200ml	7fl oz		
250ml	8fl oz	1 cup	1 cup
300ml	10fl oz/½ pint	½ pint	1¼ cups
350ml	12fl oz		
400ml	14fl oz		
450ml	15fl oz	2 cups	2 cups/1 pint
600ml	1 pint	1 pint	2½ cups
750ml	1¼ pints		
900ml	1½ pints		
1 litre	1¾ pints	1¾ pints	1 quart
1.2 litres	2 pints		
1.4 litres	2½ pints		
1.5 litres	2¾ pints		
1.7 litres	3 pints		
2 litres	3½ pints		
3 litres	5¼ pints		

UK–Australian tablespoon conversions

1 x UK or Australian teaspoon is 5ml
1 x UK tablespoon is 3 teaspoons/15ml
I Australian tablespoon is 4 teaspoons/20ml

Chicken and chorizo paella

A lovely paella that will make you dream of sunny Spain and won't break the bank.

SERVES 4
READY IN 45 MINUTES

110g cured chorizo, sliced
1 large Spanish onion, sliced
1 tbsp sweet smoked paprika
1 tsp hot paprika
3 chicken breasts, cut into large
  pieces
Knob of butter
300g paella or risotto rice
1 litre hot chicken stock
1 red pepper, sliced
Handful of green beans,
  halved
10 cherry tomatoes, halved
Handful of finely chopped
  fresh flatleaf parsley

1. Heat a large pan over a medium heat and dry-fry the chorizo until it is golden and the oil is released. Remove from the pan and set aside.

2. Add the onion to the pan and cook for 5 minutes, then stir in both the paprikas and cook for a further 2 minutes.

3. Add the chicken and cook for 3–4 minutes, then remove from the pan with the onion and set aside.

4. Heat a knob of butter in the pan and stir in the rice, then add the hot chicken stock, stir well and cook for 10 minutes.

5. Return the chorizo, chicken and onion to the pan with the red pepper, green beans and tomatoes. Season and cook for a further 5 minutes, until the rice is tender.

6. Stir the parsley into the paella and serve immediately.

★DELICIOUS. TIP Cured chorizo has a long shelf life so you don't have to use it all at once. To make this a classic risotto, cook the rice as you would for a normal risotto. Cook the other ingredients separately and add to the rice at the end with 30g grated Parmesan.

Ham and leek stovetop pasta

This is an inexpensive and homely recipe that's sure to become a favourite. Like a risotto, the pasta absorbs the flavours of the stock, ham and leeks to add depth.

SERVES 4
READY IN 25 MINUTES

300g gammon steak, trimmed of fat and cubed
1 tbsp olive oil
30g butter
3 medium leeks, washed and sliced
2 garlic cloves, crushed
2 tsp shredded fresh sage
350g dried macaroni or other small pasta shapes
1.2 litres chicken or vegetable stock, hot

1. In a large frying pan, sauté the gammon in the oil and butter until golden. Reduce the heat slightly and add the leeks. Cook, stirring, for 2 minutes, then add the garlic and sage, and cook for 1 minute.

2. Add the pasta and keep stirring around for 1–2 minutes, then pour in enough stock just to cover the pasta. Cover and simmer gently for 8–10 minutes, stirring and adding more stock as the pasta absorbs it, until it's al dente. Season and serve.

Variation Vegetarians could replace the gammon with 300g frozen Quorn pieces, thawed, and follow the recipe as normal. You can freeze for up to 1 month. Thaw but only reheat the pasta for 5 minutes so it is not overcooked.

Sausage and sweet pepper tagliatelle

This quick pasta dish with sausages and crunchy red peppers is as thrifty but as delicious as a supper gets.

SERVES 4
READY IN 20 MINUTES

400g herby sausages
280g–300g jar roasted or
   chargrilled peppers in olive oil
1 red onion
1 garlic clove, sliced
1 tsp brown sugar
3 tbsp balsamic vinegar
350g dried tagliatelle
Handful of chopped fresh
   flatleaf parsley

1. Preheat the grill to medium and cook the sausages on a foil-lined baking sheet for about 15 minutes, turning now and then, until golden brown.

2. Meanwhile, drain the peppers (reserving a little of the oil) and slice into thin strips.

3. Slice the onion and soften in a large frying pan, with 1 tablespoon of the olive oil from the pepper jar, for 5 minutes. Add the garlic, fry over a gentle heat for 1 minute, then add the peppers, brown sugar and balsamic vinegar. Cook, stirring, for a few minutes, then slice the sausages thickly, add to the pan and cook for a further 5 minutes to heat through.

4. Meanwhile, cook the tagliatelle according to the packet instructions. Season the sausage mixture with plenty of black pepper, then add the pasta to the pan with a splash of cooking water and the parsley. Divide among individual bowls or serve at the table from the pan.

Variation Make this vegetarian by using veggie sausages or adding extra veg such as chargrilled courgettes and artichokes.

Quick baked gnocchi with chorizo, spinach and mozzarella

This deliciously cheesy dish works well with any pasta shapes.
It's economical even when doubled for a family supper.

SERVES 2
TAKES 15 MINUTES, PLUS
10–15 MINUTES IN THE OVEN

500g fresh gnocchi
100g chorizo, roughly chopped
1 garlic clove, crushed
400g can chopped tomatoes
200g baby leaf spinach, washed
   and drained
125g mozzarella

1. Cook the gnocchi in salted boiling water for 2 minutes less than the packet instructions, then drain and add to a large ovenproof dish.

2. Preheat the oven to 200°C/fan 180°C/gas 6. Add the chorizo to a dry frying pan over a medium heat. Cook, stirring, for 4 minutes, until the chorizo is sizzling and browning at the edges.

3. Stir in the garlic clove, the chopped tomatoes and baby spinach. Heat through to wilt the spinach, season to taste and pour over the gnocchi in the ovenproof dish.

4. Scatter with mozzarella, torn into pieces, and bake for 10–15 minutes, until bubbling and golden.

Mushroom and bacon pasta

If you're putting bacon pieces into pasta or a risotto, don't buy expensive rashers or cubes; ask the butcher for off-cuts.

SERVES 4
READY IN 20 MINUTES

350g linguine
1 tbsp olive oil
8 rashers streaky bacon, chopped
250g chestnut mushrooms, sliced
1 tbsp fresh thyme leaves (optional)
150g frozen peas, defrosted
75ml double cream
Juice of ½ lemon
Parmesan or Grana Padano shavings, to garnish

1. Cook the pasta according to the packet instructions, drain and toss with half the olive oil and 2 tablespoons cooking water. Set aside.

2. Heat the remaining oil in a pan and fry the bacon for 5 minutes until crisp. Add the mushrooms and thyme, if using, and fry for a further 2–3 minutes.

3. Add to the pasta with the peas and warm the mixture over a low heat. Add the cream and lemon juice, and warm. Scatter with the cheese shavings and season.

Variation Turn this into a risotto: fry the bacon, mushrooms and thyme as in step 2. Add 300g risotto rice and stir. Add 900ml hot stock, a third at a time. When the rice is nearly tender, add the peas and cook. Add fresh lemon juice, 2 tablespoons Parmesan and a knob of butter.

Ravioli pasta bake

Veggies can simply leave out the chorizo slices in this otherwise vegetarian and value-for-money pasta bake.

SERVES 2
TAKES 10 MINUTES, PLUS 10 MINUTES
IN THE OVEN

250g pack fresh ricotta and spinach ravioli or tortellini
50g marinated and grilled peppers, chopped into large chunks
Handful of mixed red and yellow cherry tomatoes, halved
6 thin chorizo slices
250g pot fresh tomato sauce
½ x 125g mozzarella ball, sliced
270g garlic and herb bread
Fresh basil leaves, to garnish

1. Preheat the oven to 200°C/fan 180°C/gas 6. Tip the pasta into a 1.2-litre ovenproof dish.

2. Mix with the marinated and grilled peppers, the cherry tomatoes and the chorizo slices. Stir through the tomato sauce, thinned down with 100ml water, and scatter with the mozzarella.

3. Bake in the oven for 10 minutes, then crumble over ½ x 270g garlic and herb bread, and return to the oven for another 10 minutes, until golden and cooked through. Scatter with a few fresh basil leaves to serve.

★DELICIOUS. TIP This recipe only uses half a garlic bread, but don't waste it, freeze the other half to use with another meal.

Beef goulash with tagliatelle

This fusion dish takes beef goulash, one of the glories of Hungarian cooking, and mixes it with Italian tagliatelle to produce a warm and filling winter supper.

SERVES 4
TAKES 25 MINUTES, PLUS 1½ HOURS IN THE OVEN

500g beef stewing steak, cut into chunks
1 tbsp plain flour, seasoned
2 tbsp vegetable oil
2 onions, roughly chopped
1 garlic clove, crushed
3 tbsp paprika, plus extra to sprinkle
400g can plum tomatoes
300ml fresh beef stock, hot
142ml carton soured cream
Handful of chopped fresh curly parsley
300g dried tagliatelle
15g butter

1. Preheat the oven to 160°C/fan 140°C/gas 3. Toss the beef in the seasoned flour. Heat the vegetable oil in a large casserole over a high heat. Add half the beef and brown for 4–5 minutes. Remove and set aside. Repeat with the remaining beef.

2. Add the onions and cook, stirring, for 5 minutes. Stir in the garlic and paprika for 1 minute, then add the tomatoes, breaking them up with the spoon. Add the stock and cooked beef, bring to the boil and season.

3. Cover and bake for 1 hour. Stir and bake, uncovered, for a further 30 minutes, until the beef is tender. Stir in 100ml of the soured cream and the parsley.

4. Cook the tagliatelle according to the packet instructions. Drain and toss with the butter.

5. To serve, divide the pasta among bowls. Spoon the goulash on top, garnish with the remaining soured cream and sprinkle with extra paprika.

Beef, spinach and mozzarella ragù

This beef ragù is a perfect weeknight dish: it's quick, simple, inexpensive and satisfying.

SERVES 4
READY IN 25 MINUTES

500g pack minced beef
2 tsp olive oil
Handful of chestnut
  mushrooms, sliced
½ x 680g jar passata with
  onions and garlic
400g conchiglie (shell) pasta
Few handfuls of baby leaf
  spinach
150g mozzarella, torn

1. Stir-fry the mince in the olive oil until browned. Add the sliced chestnut mushrooms and cook for 2 minutes. Add the passata with onions and garlic, and simmer for 10–15 minutes.

2. Meanwhile, cook the pasta according to the packet instructions. Drain.

3. Stir the baby spinach and mozzarella into the ragù and cook until the cheese is just beginning to melt and the spinach is wilted.

4. Toss with the pasta. Serve immediately.

Sausage, chicken liver and porcini mushroom cannelloni

A rich and filling dish, where a little goes a long way. The perfect comfort food.

SERVES 4
TAKES 50 MINUTES, PLUS
30 MINUTES IN THE OVEN

15g dried porcini mushrooms
2 tbsp extra-virgin olive oil
1 small onion, finely chopped
2 garlic cloves, crushed
400g pack pork sausages
125g good-quality chicken
  livers, trimmed and finely
  chopped
2 tsp fresh thyme leaves
2 tbsp tomato purée
75ml chicken stock
150g (6 sheets) fresh egg
  lasagne
150g tub fresh tomato and
  mascarpone sauce
Butter, for greasing
25g Parmesan, finely grated
Fresh basil leaves, to garnish

1. Preheat the oven to 200°C/fan 180°C/gas 6. Soak the mushrooms in 100ml hot water. Heat the oil in a large pan, add the onion and garlic, and cook gently for 10 minutes, until soft and lightly browned.

2. Meanwhile, skin the sausages and break the meat into small pieces. Add to the pan and cook, breaking up the meat with a wooden spoon as it browns. Add the chicken livers and cook for 2–3 minutes. Drain the mushrooms, reserving the liquid, and chop finely. Add to the pan with the thyme and cook for 2 minutes. Stir in the tomato purée, reserved mushroom liquid and stock, and simmer for 5 minutes, until thickened.

3. Bring a large pan of salted water to the boil. Drop in the lasagne sheets, take the pan off the heat and leave to soak for 5 minutes. Drain, refresh under cold water, then separate the sheets.

4. Spoon a thin layer of the tomato sauce over the base of a buttered 20cm x 30cm ovenproof dish. Spoon the sausage filling along 1 short edge of each lasagne sheet and roll up. Put, seam-side down, on the sauce. Spoon over the remaining sauce and scatter with the Parmesan.

5. To freeze, cool, then wrap in cling film. Freeze for up to 3 months. Thaw for 24 hours in the fridge, then bring up to room temperature. To cook, bake for 30 minutes or until golden and bubbling. Serve scattered with basil leaves.

Pasticcio (Greek pasta bake)

If you thought there was nothing more delicious than moussaka – think again.

SERVES 4
TAKES 50 MINUTES, PLUS
25 MINUTES IN THE OVEN

1 tbsp olive oil, plus extra for brushing
1 large onion, finely chopped
2 garlic cloves, crushed
500g minced lamb
1 tbsp tomato purée
½ tsp ground cinnamon
400g can chopped tomatoes
2 tsp dried oregano
350g dried macaroni

For the topping
150g Greek yogurt
1 medium egg, beaten
50g mature Cheddar, grated
50g feta

1. Heat the oil in a large frying pan over a medium heat. Add the onion and garlic, and cook, stirring, for 5 minutes, until soft. Increase the heat, add the minced lamb and cook, stirring, for 5 minutes, until browned. Drain off the fat in a sieve, then return the meat and onions to the pan.

2. Add the purée and cinnamon, and cook, stirring, for 1 minute. Add the tomatoes, then half-fill the can with water and pour into the pan. Add the oregano, season, and bring to the boil. Reduce the heat and simmer, stirring occasionally, for 20 minutes.

3. Preheat the oven to 180°C/fan 160°C/gas 4. For the topping, mix the yogurt, egg and half the cheeses. Season with freshly ground black pepper.

4. Cook the macaroni in boiling water until al dente. Drain and spoon half into a deep ovenproof dish. Season. Top with the mince and remaining macaroni. Press down, spoon over the yogurt topping and scatter with the remaining cheese. Bake for 25 minutes, or until golden and bubbling.

Crispy bacon, chilli and tomato rigatoni

A quick, simple and hearty pasta dish that's a great midweek value meal for family or friends.

SERVES 4
READY IN 15 MINUTES

400g rigatoni
8 rashers streaky bacon, chopped
1 large red chilli, seeded and chopped
2 tbsp capers, rinsed
10 pitted black olives, halved
350g tub tomato pasta sauce
2 tbsp crème fraîche

1. Cook the rigatoni according to the packet instructions, then drain and reserve some water.

2. Fry the rashers in a large frying pan for 5 minutes. Add the chilli and cook for 1 minute. Add the capers, olives and tub of pasta sauce, and warm through. Stir in the crème fraîche, the pasta and reserved water. Season and serve.

Cheesy cauliflower pasta

This veggie pasta dish successfully fuses British and Italian cuisine to create affordable fare.

SERVES 4
READY IN 30 MINUTES

400g pasta shapes, such as penne
1 medium cauliflower, broken into florets
1 tbsp olive oil
Knob of butter
1 large onion, sliced
2 garlic cloves, sliced
2 tbsp chopped fresh rosemary leaves
30g grated vegetarian Parmesan
50g grated mature Cheddar
Handful of chopped fresh flatleaf parsley
Extra-virgin olive oil, to drizzle

1. Cook the pasta shapes in a pan of boiling water according to the packet instructions.

2. Meanwhile, blanch the cauliflower in a pan of boiling water for 7–8 minutes, until very tender, then drain.

3. Heat the olive oil and butter in a large pan, and fry the onion for 5 minutes, then add the garlic and chopped fresh rosemary, and cook for 2 minutes.

4. Add the cauliflower and cook for a few minutes, until golden. Break up the cauliflower, add a ladleful of the pasta water and simmer until the water evaporates.

5. Drain the pasta, add to the cauliflower mixture and toss with Parmesan, Cheddar and the parsley. Serve drizzled with extra-virgin olive oil and lots of freshly ground black pepper.

Crispy pork belly

A fantastic inexpensive cut of meat. You don't need to stick to fennel seeds on the pork belly – try adding lemon zest, garlic and rosemary instead.

SERVES 4

TAKES 10 MINUTES, 1 HOUR
20 MINUTES IN THE OVEN,
PLUS RESTING

1kg boneless pork belly, skin scored (ask your butcher to do this for you)
1 tbsp fennel seeds
1 tbsp sea salt
1 large onion, cut into wedges
3 celery sticks, cut into chunks
Seasonal vegetables, to serve

1. Preheat the oven to 190°C/fan 170°C/gas 5. Place the pork belly on a board and pat dry with kitchen paper. Rub the fennel seeds and sea salt all over the skin.

2. Place the onion wedges and celery in a roasting tin, put the pork belly on top, skin-side up, and roast for 1 hour. Increase the temperature to 220°C/fan 200°C/gas 7 and roast for a further 20 minutes, until the crackling is crisp.

3. Place on a carving board to rest for 10 minutes before slicing. Serve with seasonal vegetables.

Mexican-style pork with sweet potatoes and lime yogurt

This recipe proves that a few light ingredients go with baked sweet potatoes just as well as plain old butter and cheese.

SERVES 4

TAKES 15 MINUTES, PLUS 45 MINUTES IN THE OVEN

4 medium (about 180–200g each) sweet potatoes
150g natural yogurt
1 red chilli, seeded and finely chopped
Small bunch of fresh coriander, chopped
Finely grated zest of 1 lime, plus extra lime halves to serve
1 tsp cumin seeds
½ tsp paprika
½ tsp mild chilli powder
2 garlic cloves, crushed
1 tbsp brown sugar
1 tbsp mild olive oil
4 boneless pork loin steaks
Mixed salad, to serve (optional)

1. Preheat the oven to 180°C/fan 160°C/gas 4. Place the sweet potatoes on a baking sheet and cook for 45 minutes, until soft. Cover with foil and keep warm.

2. While they're cooking, mix the yogurt with the chilli, coriander and lime zest. Chill until needed.

3. Preheat the grill to medium. Mix the cumin, paprika, chilli powder, garlic, sugar and oil together in a large bowl. Add the pork and turn to coat. Place the pork steaks, spaced apart, in a grill pan and grill for about 6 minutes, turning halfway, until cooked but still juicy.

4. Cut the sweet potatoes into wedges and serve with the grilled pork steaks, a lime half and the yogurt on the side. Add a mixed salad, if you like.

★DELICIOUS. TIP Increase the chilli powder in the spicy pork rub if you prefer more heat or leave it out altogether for a mildly spiced steak. You can freeze the coated and uncooked pork steaks in a food bag for up to 1 month. Defrost thoroughly before grilling as in step 3.

Variation Slash some chicken breasts or drumsticks and rub the spice mixture into the flesh. Cook the chicken in the oven with the sweet potatoes for 30–45 minutes, depending on thickness.

Pork schnitzels with apple and red cabbage sauerkraut

This low-cost dish can also be made with flattened chicken or turkey breasts instead of pork.

SERVES 4
READY IN 50 MINUTES

4 x 125g pork escalopes, bashed out to about 75mm thickness
100g plain flour, seasoned
1 egg, lightly beaten
100g fresh breadcrumbs
Vegetable oil, for shallow frying
Lemon wedges, to garnish
Broccoli, to serve (optional)

For the red cabbage sauerkraut
1 tbsp olive oil
1 onion, finely sliced
600g red cabbage, cored and shredded
2 red apples, halved, cored and thinly sliced
4 tbsp white wine vinegar
2 tsp light muscovado sugar

1. Make the sauerkraut. Gently heat the oil in a large pan. Add the onion and cook for 6–8 minutes, until soft. Add the cabbage, apples, vinegar and sugar. Toss together with a pinch of salt. Cover and simmer for 30–35 minutes, stirring occasionally.

2. Meanwhile, dust each escalope with the flour and dip into the egg. Press into the breadcrumbs to coat.

3. Add 2cm vegetable oil (approximately 1.2 litres) to a frying pan and put over a medium heat. When hot, cook the pork schnitzels for 2–3 minutes on each side, until cooked through. Drain on kitchen paper and serve with the sauerkraut, lemon wedges to squeeze over and broccoli, if you like.

★DELICIOUS. TIP You can freeze the sauerkraut for up to 2 months, then thaw it and reheat it with a dash of water until hot.

Simple lamb chops with bubble and squeak cake

This is a great way to use up leftover veg from a Sunday lunch.
Use cabbage or leeks instead of sprouts, if you prefer.

SERVES 4
READY IN 45 MINUTES

50g unsalted butter, softened
2 tbsp chopped fresh flatleaf
  parsley
1 garlic clove, crushed
800g floury potatoes, cut into
  chunks
200g ready-prepared Brussels
  sprouts
5 tbsp olive oil
8 lamb chops

1. In a bowl, mix together half the butter, the parsley and garlic. Season well and set aside.

2. Place the potatoes in a saucepan of cold salted water. Bring to the boil and simmer gently for 20 minutes, until tender. Drain well and mash with the remaining butter, then allow to cool completely.

3. Meanwhile, cook the Brussels sprouts in a pan of boiling water for 6–8 minutes, until tender. Drain and refresh under cold water. Roughly chop the sprouts and mix with the cold mashed potato. Check the seasoning.

4. Heat 3 tablespoons of the olive oil in a frying pan and cook the lamb chops for 3–4 minutes each side, or until cooked to your liking.

5. Meanwhile, heat the remaining olive oil in a second frying pan and, when hot, add the bubble and squeak mixture, pressing down so it takes up the whole pan. Leave for a good 4–5 minutes, don't be tempted to stir it, then gently turn it over (you will have to do this in sections) and press down to brown the other side.

6. Add the herb butter to the pan with the chops and allow to melt, then serve with the bubble and squeak.

Variation Make extra bubble and squeak cakes, and serve with fried bacon and poached eggs for a delicious breakfast.

Braised pork chops with lentils

A deliciously tender way to eat pork. The meat and lentils go well together in this inexpensive dish – lentils are a fantastic source of dietary fibre and pork is quite naturally low in fat.

SERVES 4
TAKES 20 MINUTES, PLUS
40–45 MINUTES IN THE OVEN

2 tbsp olive oil
1 onion, chopped
2 garlic cloves, crushed
4 pork chops, dusted in 1 tbsp
  plain seasoned flour
1 fresh rosemary sprig
2 fresh thyme sprigs
400ml cider or chicken stock
150g Puy lentils
Chopped fresh parsley, to
  garnish
Soured cream, to serve

1. Preheat the oven to 180°C/fan 160°C/gas 4. Heat 1 tablespoon olive oil in a large frying pan over a low heat, and fry the onion and garlic for 5 minutes. Add to a flameproof casserole.

2. Heat another 1 tablespoon olive oil in the frying pan and brown the pork chops for 2–3 minutes each side. Add the chops to the casserole along with the fresh rosemary sprig and fresh thyme sprigs, and season well.

3. Pour over the cider or chicken stock, bring to a simmer, then cover and cook in the oven for 20 minutes.

4. Add the Puy lentils to the casserole and return to the oven, uncovered, to cook for a further 20–25 minutes, until the lentils are tender and most of the liquid has been absorbed. Season and serve scattered with some chopped fresh parsley and a dollop of soured cream.

Variation Here's a quick idea: cube the pork chop meat and fry with the onion and garlic, add a splash of chicken stock and ½ tub half-fat crème fraîche, and serve with cooked lentils.

Pork goulash with paprika yogurt

A quick and simple pork recipe with a kick but no strain on your purse.

SERVES 4
READY IN 20 MINUTES

4 pork loin steaks
2 tsp paprika, plus extra
  to sprinkle
2 tsp olive oil
400g can chopped tomatoes
  with herbs
560g can peeled new potatoes
  in water, drained and larger
  ones halved
Handful of chopped fresh
  flatleaf parsley
75g natural yogurt, plus extra
  to serve
Crusty bread, to serve

1. Trim the pork loin steaks of excess fat, cut into 2cm cubes and toss with the paprika and some seasoning.

2. Heat a wide frying pan over a medium–high heat, add the olive oil and the pork, and cook for 2-3 minutes, until browned.

3. Add the tomatoes with herbs and a dash of water. Bring to the boil, stir in the potatoes. Reduce the heat slightly and simmer rapidly for 5 minutes or until the pork and potatoes are tender and the sauce reduced a little. Season.

4. Cool slightly, then stir in the parsley and yogurt. Divide the goulash among 4 wide bowls, top each with a spoonful of natural yogurt and sprinkle with paprika.

5. Serve with crusty bread to mop up the sauce.

Easy lamb tagine

A great recipe for raiding the storecupboard and using cheap ingredients you already have.

SERVES 4
READY IN ABOUT 1 HOUR

400g lamb leg steaks, cubed
2 tbsp olive oil
1 onion, sliced
2 garlic cloves, chopped
2 tsp ground coriander
2 tsp ground cumin
1 tsp ground ginger
Pinch of ground cinnamon
400g can chopped tomatoes
200ml chicken stock, hot
100g pitted prunes, chopped
1 tbsp ground almonds
Handful of chopped fresh
  coriander
Herby couscous, to serve
  (see tip)

1. Brown the lamb leg steaks in the olive oil in a pan. Set aside. Add the onion and garlic to the pan, and fry for 5 minutes.

2. Add the ground coriander, cumin, ginger and cinnamon, and fry for 2 minutes.

3. Add the lamb, chopped tomatoes and chicken stock. Add the prunes. Simmer for 40–45 minutes.

4. Stir in the ground almonds and fresh coriander. Serve with herby couscous.

★DELICIOUS. TIP Soak 250g couscous in 300ml boiling water for 5 minutes. Add plenty of seasoning, lemon zest and juice and lots of chopped fresh parsley and mint.

Variation This works just as well with diced turkey breast. Cook in the same way but only simmer for 20-30 minutes.

Sweet and sticky gammon with stir-fried vegetables

A delicious and good-value meal – you can easily double the recipe to serve four.

SERVES 2
READY IN ABOUT 15 MINUTES

2 large gammon steaks
Pinch of Chinese five spice
  powder
2 tbsp olive oil
1 tbsp clear honey
1 tbsp mandarin marmalade
1 lime, halved, and 1 half cut
  into wedges to serve
300g bag mixed stir-fry
  vegetables
½ red cabbage, cored and
  shredded
2 tsp white wine vinegar
½ tsp caster sugar

1. Season the gammon steaks and dust with a good pinch of Chinese five spice powder. Heat 1 tablespoon olive oil in a pan over a medium–high heat, add the steaks and cook for 3 minutes each side, until the rind is crisp.

2. Add the honey, mandarin marmalade and a squeeze of lime to the pan. Bubble for a couple of minutes, turning the steaks until coated, sticky and cooked through. Remove to a plate to rest.

3. Pour another tablespoon olive oil into the pan, add the stir-fry vegetables and red cabbage. Cook for 2 minutes, then stir through the white wine vinegar, caster sugar and a good squeeze of lime.

4. Season and toss around the pan for 1 minute. Spoon between plates, serve the gammon steaks alongside and garnish with extra lime wedges.

Spicy corned beef hash with egg

Add a softly fried egg and chilli to this cheap and cheerful
favourite to make a spicy and filling supper.

SERVES 4
READY IN 40 MINUTES

3 tbsp vegetable oil
900g white potatoes, diced
1 onion, chopped
340g can corned beef, chopped
1 red chilli, seeded and sliced
Handful of chopped fresh curly
   parsley
4 medium eggs

1. Heat 2 tablespoons of the oil in a large frying
pan over a medium heat. Add the potatoes and
cook, stirring occasionally, for 15 minutes, until
lightly browned.

2. Add the chopped onion and cook for 10 minutes,
until the onion is softened and the potatoes
are golden.

3. Stir in the corned beef and sliced red chilli, and
cook for 6–8 minutes, until the hash is crispy in
places. Stir in the parsley and season to taste.

4. Meanwhile, heat the remaining oil in a second
frying pan over a medium heat. Crack in the eggs
and cook for 4–5 minutes, until the whites are set
and the yolks are hot but runny. To serve, divide
the hash among the plates and top each with a
fried egg.

Apricot-stuffed lamb shoulder with rosemary roast potatoes

A good-value Sunday lunch. The apricot stuffing gives a lovely, fruity flavour to the lamb.

SERVES 4, PLUS LEFTOVERS
FOR COLD CUTS
TAKES 20 MINUTES, 1 HOUR
10 MINUTES IN THE OVEN,
PLUS RESTING

3 tbsp vegetable oil
About 900g boned shoulder of lamb (roughly 1.2kg bone-in)
900g white potatoes, halved or quartered
Leaves from 1 fresh rosemary sprig, plus extra to garnish
1 tbsp plain flour
450ml fresh beef stock, hot

For the apricot stuffing
125g dried ready-to-eat apricots, chopped
75g fresh white breadcrumbs
Leaves from 3 fresh rosemary sprigs, chopped
Grated zest and juice of 1 lemon

1. Preheat the oven to 200°C/fan 180°C/gas 6. Put 2 tablespoons of the oil in a large roasting tin and pop in the oven to heat up. Mix the stuffing ingredients together in a bowl and season well with salt and pepper.

2. Season the lamb and lay on a board, boned-out side up. Spread with the stuffing, leaving a small border all around. Roll up the lamb and tie up with kitchen string to secure.

3. Add the potatoes to the hot roasting tin, toss in the oil then nestle the lamb among them. Rub the lamb with the remaining oil. Roast for 1 hour, turning the potatoes after 45 minutes.

4. Scatter the rosemary over the potatoes and roast for a further 10 minutes, until the potatoes are golden and the lamb is still pink. Lift the lamb and potatoes on to plates, cover and set aside.

5. Make a gravy. Tip off most of the fat from the roasting tin. Put on the hob over a high heat, add the flour and stir for 30 seconds. Gradually stir in the stock, then boil for 3–4 minutes, until thickened. Season.

6. Carve the lamb. Divide among plates with the potatoes. Serve with the gravy and seasonal vegetables, garnished with rosemary, if you like.

Cauliflower cheese with ham

Add some ham to this comforting and cost-conscious classic dish to give it some extra flavour.

SERVES 4
READY IN 20 MINUTES

1 large (about 1.3kg) cauliflower
25g butter
25g plain flour
568ml carton semi-skimmed milk
150g mature Cheddar, grated
3 tbsp wholegrain mustard
6 thin slices cooked ham, sliced

1. Cut the cauliflower into florets, reserving the small green leaves. Cook in a pan of boiling, lightly salted water for 8 minutes, until just tender. Add the leaves and cook for a further 2 minutes. Drain well and tip into a deep 2-litre heatproof dish.

2. Meanwhile, preheat the grill to high. Make the sauce. Melt the butter in a pan over a medium heat. Add the flour and cook, stirring, for 1 minute. Gradually stir in the milk, bring up to a simmer and cook, stirring, until thickened. Stir in 100g of the cheese, the mustard and half the ham. Season with freshly ground black pepper.

3. Pour the sauce over the cauliflower and scatter with the remaining cheese and ham. Pop under the grill for 3–4 minutes, until the cheese is melted and golden.

Ham hock, split pea and mint stew

This budget cut of ham hock goes well with split peas and potatoes, while the mint freshens up the stew.

SERVES 4
READY IN ABOUT 2 HOURS

600g ham hock
2 carrots, roughly chopped
1 large onion, quartered
6 black peppercorns
150g dried yellow split peas
450g white potatoes, cut into cubes
150g frozen peas
Small handful of chopped fresh mint, to garnish

1. Put the ham hock, carrots, onion and peppercorns in a large pan. Add 1.7 litres water, cover, and bring to the boil. Reduce the heat slightly and simmer for 1 hour. Skim off any scum.

2. Strain the cooking liquid through a colander into another large pan. Set the hock aside to cool slightly, then pull off the meat and shred. Cover and set aside. Discard the bone and the contents of the colander.

3. Bring the liquid to a simmer. Add the split peas and cook for 35 minutes, skimming off any scum. Add the potatoes and cook for 10–12 minutes or until the potatoes and split peas are tender. Stir in the frozen peas and cook for 2–3 minutes, until soft. Take off the heat and stir in most of the mint. Blend half until smooth, mix with the remainder and season.

4. Divide the stew among warmed bowls. Top with the shredded ham and reserved mint to serve.

★DELICIOUS. TIP Buy ham hocks from your butcher for around £2.50 each.

Lancashire hotpot

A popular dish with families, this traditional English recipe is cheap to make and always satisfying.

SERVES 4

TAKES 25 MINUTES, PLUS 50 MINUTES IN THE OVEN

1 tbsp olive oil
500g lamb leg steaks, cubed
2 tbsp plain seasoned flour
1 large onion, sliced
2 small carrots, sliced
300ml hot chicken stock
1 tbsp Worcestershire sauce
Few fresh thyme sprigs
600g waxy potatoes
Butter, for dotting

1. Preheat the oven to 190°C/fan 170°C/gas 5. Heat the olive oil in a large, wide pan over a medium heat. Dust the lamb leg steaks in the seasoned flour and fry, in batches, until browned. Set aside.

2. Add the onion to the pan with the carrots, and cook for 5 minutes. Return the lamb to the pan with the hot chicken stock, Worcestershire sauce and the thyme. Season and remove from the heat.

3. Thinly slice the potatoes and place half in an overlapping layer in a shallow ovenproof pan. Top with the meat mixture, then layer over the remaining potato and dot with butter. Cover and cook in the oven for 30 minutes, then remove the lid and cook for a further 20 minutes, until the potatoes are golden brown.

Variation Turn this into a shepherd's pie: cut the lamb into very small pieces, add 2 tablespoons each of tomato ketchup and tomato purée with the Worcestershire sauce and stock, then top with mash.

Pearl barley, bacon and leek casserole

Perfect for a cold evening, this is a savvy and warming dish that will become favourite comfort food.

SERVES 4
READY IN JUST OVER 1 HOUR

Knob of butter
1 tbsp olive oil
250g piece of bacon or pork belly, cut into pieces
2 leeks, thickly sliced
2 garlic cloves, crushed
300g pearl barley
300g peeled and cubed butternut squash
3 tbsp fresh thyme leaves
1 litre chicken stock, hot
175g self-raising flour
75g butter
75g Cheddar, grated
2 tbsp chopped fresh flatleaf parsley

1. Heat a large pan over a medium heat. Add a good knob of butter and the olive oil and fry the bacon or pork belly for 5 minutes, until golden.

2. Add the leeks and garlic, and fry for a few minutes. Add the pearl barley, butternut squash, fresh thyme leaves, and chicken stock. Season. Simmer for 25 minutes until the barley is nearly tender.

3. In a bowl, mix the self-raising flour with the butter, Cheddar, parsley, some seasoning and a splash of water until it forms a soft dough. Roll into walnut-sized dumplings, add to the casserole and cook for a further 10–15 minutes. Serve immediately.

Sticky ribs with whipped potatoes

Re-create American-style diner food at home.

SERVES 4
READY IN ABOUT 50 MINUTES

1.2kg spare ribs
800g floury potatoes
200g tub of light cream cheese
  with garlic and herbs
100ml milk, warmed
275g bottle of honeyed
  barbecue sauce
Steamed green beans, to serve
  (optional)

1. Cover the spare ribs with cold water in a large saucepan and bring to the boil. Reduce the heat, cover partially and simmer gently for 30 minutes. Drain in a colander. Preheat the grill to medium.

2. Meanwhile, put the potatoes in a pan, cover with cold salted water and bring to the boil over a medium heat. Reduce the temperature slightly and simmer for 12–15 minutes or until tender. Drain well and mash until smooth. Season well and beat in the cream cheese and milk using a wooden spoon. Continue to beat vigorously until light and fluffy. Cover and keep warm.

3. Spread the ribs out in a single layer in a foil-lined roasting tin. Pour over the honeyed barbecue sauce and grill for 15 minutes, turning every 3 minutes, until golden and sticky.

4. Serve with a generous spoonful of mash and some steamed green beans, if you like.

Mexican minced beef and spicy polenta cobbler

Don't let the long list of ingredients put you off – this is a simple and inexpensive dish that's ideal for feeding a crowd.

SERVES 8
TAKES 1 HOUR, PLUS 20 MINUTES IN THE OVEN

4 tbsp sunflower oil
3 medium onions, finely chopped
4 garlic cloves, crushed
1 tsp crushed dried chillies
2 tsp freshly ground cumin seeds
1kg lean minced beef
3 tbsp tomato purée
1½ tbsp light muscovado sugar
2 tsp dried oregano
300ml beef stock, hot
200g can chopped tomatoes
2 roasted red peppers from a jar, drained
400g can red kidney beans in water, drained and rinsed

For the spicy polenta cobbler
200g plain flour
1 tbsp baking powder
1 tbsp brown soft sugar
¼ tsp crushed dried chillies
75g polenta
65g Cheddar, finely grated
1 medium egg
175ml milk
2 tbsp sunflower oil
25g butter, melted

1. Heat the oil in a large pan, add the onions and garlic, and cook for 10 minutes, until lightly browned. Add the chillies and cumin, and fry for 2–3 minutes. Add the beef and cook over a high heat, breaking up with a wooden spoon as it browns. Add the purée, sugar, oregano, beef stock and tomatoes, bring to the boil, then simmer for 25 minutes, until reduced and thickened.

2. Finely chop the peppers and stir into the meat with the kidney beans. Season, then spoon into a 2.75–3-litre shallow, oval ovenproof dish.

3. Preheat the oven to 220°C/fan 200°C/gas 7. Make the cobbler. Sift the flour, baking powder and a pinch of salt into a large mixing bowl, add the sugar and stir in the chillies, polenta and 50g grated cheese. Beat the egg, milk, oil and melted butter together, and stir into the dry ingredients.

4. Drop 8 spoonfuls of the mixture around the edge of the dish, about 2.5cm apart, and sprinkle with the remaining grated cheese. Bake for 20 minutes, until the beef is bubbling and the topping is puffed up and golden.

Meatloaf

Meatloaf is a nutritious, filling meal that kids will love; and because it uses inexpensive ingredients, it will be popular with mum too.

SERVES 4
TAKES 15 MINUTES, 1½–1¾ HOURS
IN THE OVEN, PLUS COOLING

Vegetable oil, for greasing
700g minced beef or
  500g minced beef and
  200g minced pork
2 onions, finely chopped
2 garlic cloves, crushed
1 large carrot, grated
2 tsp dried thyme
1 egg, lightly beaten
250g fresh breadcrumbs
50ml milk
2 tbsp Worcestershire sauce
2 tsp Dijon mustard
Mashed potatoes, gravy and
  mixed veg, to serve

1. Preheat the oven to 160°C/fan 140°C/gas 3. Grease a 900g loaf tin. In a bowl, mix the mince, onions, garlic, carrot, thyme and egg. Meanwhile, in a separate bowl, mix the breadcrumbs with the milk, then add to the meat mixture. Stir in the Worcestershire sauce and mustard, and season well.

2. Fill the loaf tin with the mixture. Cover with foil. Put in a deep roasting tin and pour in boiling water to come a third of the way up the loaf tin's sides. Bake for 1½–1¾ hours, until cooked through. Cool for 15 minutes in the tin, then remove, slice and serve with mashed potato, gravy and mixed vegetables.

★DELICIOUS. TIP Freeze the cooled meatloaf for up to 3 months. Thaw, slice and microwave until hot.

Curried minced lamb cobbler

Warm up the winter months with this lightly spiced twist on a classic English cobbler.

SERVES 4
TAKES 50 MINUTES, PLUS
15–25 MINUTES IN THE OVEN

1 tbsp olive oil
1 large onion, finely chopped
1 tbsp mild or medium curry powder
500g minced lamb
450g swede, cubed
3 tbsp mango chutney, plus extra to serve
400ml fresh lamb stock, hot
Seasonal vegetables, to serve

For the cobbler
225g self-raising flour
60g cold butter, cut into cubes
1 tsp cumin seeds (optional)
1 medium egg
125ml milk

1. Heat the oil in a large, deep frying pan over a medium heat. Add the onion and cook for 5 minutes, stirring occasionally, until soft. Stir in the curry powder and cook for 1 minute. Increase the heat, add the mince and cook for 5 minutes, breaking it up with the spoon, until browned.

2. Stir in the swede, chutney and stock, and bring to a simmer. Cook for 20 minutes, stirring, until the swede is tender. Season and tip into 4 x 500ml ovenproof dishes or a deep 2-litre ovenproof dish.

3. Preheat the oven to 190°C/fan 170°C/gas 5. Make the cobbler. Sift the flour and a good pinch of salt into a bowl. Add the butter and rub in with your fingertips to coarse crumbs. Stir in the cumin, if using. Beat the egg with the milk, add to the flour mixture and mix to a firm dough. Dot clumps on top of the mince, spaced apart.

4. Bake for 15–20 minutes for individual dishes or 25 minutes for the large dish. Serve with extra chutney and seasonal vegetables.

Variation You can make a more British version of this dish by omitting the curry powder and chutney. Instead, flavour the mince with tomato purée and Worcestershire sauce. Add chopped thyme instead of cumin to flavour the cobbler.

Keema pie

The word 'keema' means Indian or spiced minced meat.
This is traditionally served like a curry, but here it is used in
a spicy shepherd's pie to make a hearty midweek meal.

SERVES 4
TAKES 30 MINUTES, PLUS
20 MINUTES IN THE OVEN

1 tbsp sunflower oil
1 red onion, finely chopped
2 garlic cloves, finely chopped
1 red chilli, seeded and
  finely chopped
Knob of fresh ginger, chopped
1 tsp cumin seeds
2 ripe tomatoes, roughly
  chopped
500g lean minced beef
2 tbsp madras curry paste
150ml chicken stock, hot
200g frozen peas
Juice of 1 lime
Mango chutney, to serve

For the mash
1kg sweet potatoes, cubed
4 tbsp soured cream
4 tbsp snipped fresh chives

1. Make the mash. Cook the sweet potatoes in a
pan of boiling, lightly salted water for 15 minutes,
until tender. Drain well, mash with the soured
cream, some seasoning and the chives.

2. Meanwhile, heat the oil in a large frying pan
over a medium heat. Add the onion, garlic, chilli
and ginger, and cook, stirring occasionally, for
6–8 minutes, until golden. Add the cumin seeds,
cook for 1 minute, then stir in the tomatoes, mince
and curry paste, and cook for 5 minutes, until the
tomatoes are pulpy. Add the stock and simmer for
10 minutes.

3. Preheat the oven to 200°C/fan 180°C/gas 6. Stir
the peas and lime juice into the keema mix and
season. Spoon into an ovenproof dish and top with
the mash, roughing it up slightly.

4. Transfer the dish to a baking sheet and bake for
20 minutes, until the top is lightly browned. Serve
with mango chutney.

★DELICIOUS. TIP Freeze it at the end of step 3 for
up to 3 months. Defrost thoroughly and bring to
room temperature before baking.

Quick cottage pie

Turn a tin of budget baked beans into a much loved supper; this recipe can be easily doubled for friends.

SERVES 2
READY IN 15 MINUTES

250g good-quality minced beef
1 small onion, chopped
415g can baked beans in tomato
  sauce
2 tbsp Worcestershire sauce
1 tsp dried mixed herbs
450g pack ready-made
  mashed potato, chilled
Cooked peas, to serve (optional)

1. Heat a large, dry frying pan over a high heat. Add the mince and onion, and cook, stirring, to break up the meat, for 3–4 minutes, until the meat is browned.

2. Stir in the baked beans, Worcestershire sauce, mixed herbs, some seasoning and a good dash of water. Simmer rapidly for 3–4 minutes, until thickened. Tip into a deep 1.2-litre baking dish.

3. Meanwhile, preheat the grill to high. Heat the mashed potato according to the packet instructions, spoon on top of the mince and rough up the surface. Pop under the hot grill for a few minutes, until golden and bubbling.

4. Serve with cooked peas, if you like.

Szechuan pork

This dish takes its name from the peppercorns used in the dish and has a lovely mild oriental flavour.

SERVES 4
READY IN 25 MINUTES

1 tbsp groundnut oil
2 shallots, finely sliced
2.5cm piece fresh ginger, sliced,
  plus extra to serve
1 red chilli, seeded and
  finely chopped, plus extra
  to serve
500g minced pork
2 tsp Szechuan peppercorns,
  crushed
1 tsp Chinese five spice
2 tbsp soy sauce
1 tbsp honey
Juice of 1 lime
350g basmati rice
165ml can coconut milk
2 tbsp chopped fresh coriander
Finely sliced spring onions,
  to garnish

1. Heat the groundnut oil in a pan or wok and fry the shallots with the ginger and chilli for a couple of minutes.

2. Add the mince and quickly brown, then stir in the peppercorns and Chinese five spice, and cook for a couple of minutes. Add the soy sauce, honey and lime juice, and cook for 5 minutes more.

3. Meanwhile, cook the basmati rice in a pan of boiling salted water for 10 minutes. Drain and return to the pan over a low heat with the coconut milk until it is absorbed.

4. Stir the coriander into the mince and serve on a bed of coconut rice. Garnish with some finely sliced spring onions, chilli and fresh ginger.

Variation If you don't have Szechuan peppercorns or five spice powder, add 1–2 tablespoons teriyaki or hoisin sauce instead and a dash of sweet chilli sauce for heat, if liked.

Pork burgers with sweet potato wedges

This is really simple, hearty food for minimum effort and expense, but maximum taste.

SERVES 4
TAKES 20 MINUTES, PLUS
30–40 MINUTES IN THE OVEN

3-4 sweet potatoes, cut into
  wedges
4 tbsp olive oil
1 small red onion, finely
  chopped
500g minced pork
1 apple, peeled and grated
½ tsp chilli flakes
4 ciabatta rolls
Pickled beetroot, mayo and
  salad leaves, to garnish

1. Preheat the oven to 200°C/fan 180°C/gas 6. Put the sweet potatoes on a baking sheet. Drizzle with 2 tablespoons of the oil, season and cook in the oven for 30–40 minutes, until golden.

2. Meanwhile, heat 1 tablespoon olive oil in a frying pan over a low heat and fry the onion for 5 minutes, until tender. Cool and mix in a bowl with the mince, apple, and chilli flakes. Season and shape into patties. (You can freeze the uncooked pork burgers for up to 3 months in a plastic container. Defrost thoroughly before cooking.) Cook in 1 tablespoon of olive oil in the frying pan over a medium heat for 5–6 minutes each side or until cooked.

3. Serve in ciabatta rolls with pickled beetroot, mayo, salad leaves and the wedges.

★DELICIOUS. TIP Adding apple to burgers and meatballs gives a natural sweetness, that cuts down on artificial sugars.

Lamb karahi

For Asian dishes that use a lot of spices, choose supermarket-own brands, rather than premium names – it's a great way to make savings. Or bulk-buy spices from local Asian shops.

SERVES 4
READY IN 35 MINUTES

2 tbsp olive oil
1 large onion, sliced
2 garlic cloves, crushed
2 tsp each cumin seeds, ground coriander and garam masala
1 tsp chilli flakes
400g lamb leg steaks, cut into cubes
400g can chopped tomatoes
Handful of chopped fresh coriander
Dollop of natural yogurt and naan bread or steamed basmati rice, to serve

1. Heat the olive oil in a large pan and gently fry the onion and garlic cloves for 5 minutes, until soft.

2. Add the cumin seeds, ground coriander, garam masala and chilli flakes, and cook for 1 minute.

3. Add the lamb leg steaks and brown all over. Pour in the chopped tomatoes, add a splash of water and simmer for 15–20 minutes.

4. Stir in a handful of chopped fresh coriander and serve with a dollop of natural yogurt and naan bread or steamed basmati rice.

Variation For a delicious mild curry, follow the recipe but cook the lamb and spices with a few crushed cardamom pods for an extra 15 minutes. Replace the tomatoes with a 200g tub natural yogurt and 2 tablespoons ground almonds, and cook for 5 more minutes.

Lentil and tomato dhal with lamb koftas

Mildly spiced lamb dhals make wonderfully cheap and filling suppers; this recipe will feed four for less than £3.50.

SERVES 4
TAKES 40 MINUTES, PLUS CHILLING

1 tbsp sunflower oil
1 onion, chopped
1 garlic clove, finely chopped
3cm piece fresh ginger, grated
½ tsp ground turmeric
200g split red lentils, washed and drained
800ml vegetable or chicken stock, hot
400g can of chopped tomatoes
1 tbsp garam masala
100g baby leaf spinach, washed
Mango chutney, to serve

For the koftas
1 small onion, grated
1 garlic clove, crushed
3cm piece fresh ginger, grated
1 tsp curry powder
400g lean lamb mince

1. Mix all the kofta ingredients in a bowl. Mould tablespoonfuls around the end of 12 metal or wooden skewers (if using wooden skewers, soak them in water for 20 minutes first). Chill for 30 minutes to firm up.

2. Meanwhile, heat the oil in a pan over a medium heat. Add the onion and cook for 5 minutes, until soft. Stir in the garlic and ginger and cook for 1 minute. Add the turmeric and lentils and stir well. Pour in half the stock, bring to the boil, then simmer for 5 minutes. Stir in the can of chopped tomatoes, add the remaining stock, cover and simmer for 10 minutes, until the lentils are tender.

3. Meanwhile, heat a griddle pan and cook the koftas for 8–10 minutes, turning, until cooked. Keep warm.

4. Add the garam masala, ½ teaspoon salt and spinach to the dhal and stir until the spinach wilts. Serve with the koftas and some mango chutney.

Variation Make the koftas with minced turkey, pork or beef, and shape into meatballs or turn the mixture into burgers.

Lamb tikka with spiced carrot salad in flatbread

A quick, easy and economical lamb recipe – this supper beats the takeaway version hands down.

SERVES 4
TAKES 20 MINUTES, PLUS MARINATING

3 tbsp natural yogurt
4cm piece fresh ginger, finely grated
2 tsp curry powder
4 lamb leg steaks, cut into large cubes
1 tsp olive oil
2 tsp black mustard seeds
2 medium carrots, coarsely grated
Finely grated zest and juice of 1 lime
100g cherry tomatoes, halved
Small handful of fresh coriander, roughly chopped (optional)
1 tbsp extra-virgin olive oil
4 round flatbreads, chapatis or pitta breads and tomato relish or chutney, to serve

1. Mix the yogurt, ginger and curry powder together in a large bowl. Add the lamb cubes, turn to coat, then leave to marinate for 10 minutes.

2. Heat the oil in a frying pan, add the mustard seeds and cook over a medium heat until they begin to pop. Remove from the heat and transfer to a large bowl. Stir in the carrots, lime zest and juice, tomatoes and coriander, if using, with the extra-virgin olive oil and salt and pepper to taste.

3. Preheat the grill to medium and thread the lamb on to 4 skewers (see tip). Lay the skewers on a baking sheet lined with foil. Season and grill for 4 minutes, turning halfway, until cooked but still juicy.

4. Spoon the carrot salad on to the flatbreads, top with the lamb and some relish or chutney and roll up to eat.

★DELICIOUS. TIP If you are using wooden skewers, soak them in cold water for at least 20 minutes before using to minimize scorching. You can freeze the marinated lamb in an airtight container for up to 1 month. Thaw before threading on to skewers and grilling as instructed in step 3.

Variation Use cubed chicken breast for a more traditional tikka, and serve with naan bread and cucumber raita.

Baked mushrooms with sausage, bacon and tomato

Delicious, breakfast-inspired baked mushrooms that could be eaten at any time of day.

SERVES 6

TAKES 15 MINUTES, 20 MINUTES IN THE OVEN, PLUS OVERNIGHT CHILLING

6 very large field mushrooms
75g butter, at room temperature, plus extra for greasing
1 heaped tbsp chopped fresh thyme leaves
4 pork and herb sausages, skinned
100g smoked bacon lardons
1 beef tomato, cut into small dice
6 tbsp coarsely grated Cheddar

1. The night before, remove the mushroom stalks and chop finely. Clean the caps and place gill-side up in a lightly greased roasting tin. Mix the butter, thyme and some seasoning, and spread over each one. Scatter with the chopped stalks.

2. Pull the sausagemeat into small pieces and pile on to the mushrooms with the lardons and tomato. Season lightly, cover and chill overnight.

3. The next morning, preheat the oven to 190°C/fan 170°C/gas 5. Bake for 15 minutes or until the bacon and sausage are lightly golden and the mushrooms have softened. Remove, sprinkle each mushroom with cheese and bake for a further 5 minutes.

★DELICIOUS. TIP Each mushroom should be 11–12cm across – if you can't get them this big, serve 2 each.

Sticky sausage and lentil stew

A flavour-packed meaty dinner to chase off the winter blues.

SERVES 4
READY IN 35 MINUTES

1 tbsp olive oil
8 pork chipolata sausages
1 onion, chopped
150g Chantenay carrots,
    quartered lengthways
2 parsnips, quartered
    lengthways
150g field mushrooms, roughly
    chopped
2 tsp Marmite
1 heaped tbsp runny honey
250ml dark ale
250g ready-cooked Puy lentils
Chopped fresh flatleaf parsley,
    to garnish
Crusty bread, to serve

1. Heat the olive oil in a heavy-based pan and brown the sausages on all sides, then remove and set aside.

2. Add the onion, carrots and parsnips to the pan. Fry for 8 minutes until golden brown and softened. Add the mushrooms and cook for 2 minutes more.

3. Return the sausages to the pan and stir through the Marmite and runny honey. Pour over the dark ale, bring to a simmer and add the Puy lentils. Bubble for 5 minutes until sticky, then check the seasoning. Scatter with chopped fresh flatleaf parsley and serve with crusty bread.

Variation This would also work well with spicy sausages or even vegetarian ones.

Toad-in-the-hole with red onions and quick gravy

A British favourite, with its succulent sausages and comforting batter. It's always a winner.

SERVES 4

TAKES 20 MINUTES, PLUS
20–25 MINUTES IN THE OVEN

250g plain flour, plus 1 tbsp
4 eggs, lightly beaten
300ml milk
4 tbsp sunflower or light olive oil
8 (about 500g) sausages
3 red onions, each cut into
   8 wedges
2 tbsp fresh thyme leaves
100ml red wine
450ml chicken stock, hot
Wholegrain mustard and
   steamed greens, to serve
   (optional)

1. Preheat the oven to 220°C/fan 200°C/gas 7. Sift the flour and ½ teaspoon salt into a bowl. Make a well in the centre, add the eggs and milk, and whisk to a smooth batter.

2. Heat 1 tablespoon of the oil in a large frying pan over a medium heat and add the sausages. Brown for 5 minutes, turning regularly, then remove and set aside. Add the onions to the pan and cook for a further 8 minutes, adding the thyme halfway through. Set aside.

3. Pour the remaining oil into a medium ovenproof dish and heat in the oven for 5 minutes. Arrange the sausages and onions in the dish, then pour over the batter. Bake for 20–25 minutes, until puffed up and golden.

4. Meanwhile, put the frying pan back over a medium–high heat, sprinkle in the extra flour and stir for 30 seconds. Gradually whisk in the red wine, then the chicken stock. Bubble for about 5 minutes to reduce the gravy by half. Keep warm over a very low heat.

5. Serve the toad-in-the-hole with the hot gravy, a dollop of wholegrain mustard and some steamed greens, if you like.

★DELICIOUS. TIP For vegetarians, use veggie sausages and vegetable stock instead.

Frankfurter and mushroom tortilla

Frugal favourite frankfurters aren't just for hot dogs; try them in this delicious tortilla dish instead.

SERVES 4
READY IN 25 MINUTES

1 tbsp vegetable oil
350g frankfurters, cut into chunks
1 onion, finely sliced
200g white mushrooms, sliced
6 large eggs
2 slices white bread, torn into pieces
Good handful of fresh curly parsley, chopped, plus extra to garnish
Green salad, to serve

1. Heat the oil in a 23cm heavy-based, ovenproof frying pan over a medium heat. Add the frankfurters and cook for 3–4 minutes, stirring, until golden. Remove and set aside.

2. Add the onion to the pan and cook, stirring, for 5 minutes, until softened. Add the mushrooms, cook for 3–4 minutes, then stir in the frankfurters.

3. Meanwhile, preheat the grill to high. Beat the eggs in a bowl with 3 tablespoons of water. Add the bread and parsley, and season. Pour into the frying pan and cook over a medium–low heat for 8 minutes or until just set and golden underneath.

4. Pop the pan under the grill for 2–3 minutes, to brown the top slightly. Scatter with the extra parsley, cut into quarters and serve with a green salad.

Variation Bacon or cooked sausages would also work well. For vegetarians, use 1 sliced courgette instead of the frankfurters.

Oven-baked sausages and balsamic tomatoes

This colourful and comforting dish is full of the flavours of the Mediterranean.

SERVES 4
TAKES 5 MINUTES, PLUS 30 MINUTES IN THE OVEN

12 sausages
6 garlic cloves, sliced
2 red onions, cut into wedges
A little olive oil
600g cherry tomatoes, halved
3 tbsp balsamic vinegar
Handful of torn fresh
  basil leaves

1. Preheat the oven to 200°C/fan 180°C/gas 6. In a large roasting tin, toss together the sausages, garlic and red onions with a little olive oil.

2. Put in the oven and roast for 15 minutes, until golden. Add the cherry tomatoes and balsamic vinegar. Season and toss together gently.

3. Return to the oven for a further 15 minutes, stir in the basil leaves and serve.

chicken and poultry

Sicilian turkey meatballs and pasta

This Italian family favourite with meatballs and pasta is quick to make and easy on your waistline and purse.

SERVES 4
READY IN 25 MINUTES

500g minced turkey
50g fresh breadcrumbs
50g sultanas or raisins
1 garlic clove, crushed
Grated zest of 1 lemon
Pinch of dried chilli flakes
Small bunch of fresh flatleaf
  parsley, leaves chopped
1 tbsp olive oil
250ml chicken stock, hot
350g dried spaghetti

1. Combine the minced turkey in a bowl with the breadcrumbs, dried fruit, garlic, lemon zest, chilli, half the parsley and plenty of seasoning. Form into about 20 small meatballs.

2. Heat the oil in a large frying pan and add the meatballs. Cook for about 4 minutes, turning frequently, until golden. Add the stock and turn up the heat. Simmer briskly for 5 minutes, until the stock is reduced by half. Turn off the heat.

3. Meanwhile, cook the spaghetti according to the packet instructions. Drain the pasta, return it to the saucepan and add the meatballs and sauce, along with the remaining parsley. Season, toss well and serve.

★DELICIOUS. TIP Freeze at the end of step 2 for up to 3 months. Thaw, reheat until piping hot and finish the recipe.

Variation Try using lean minced pork and the leaves from a few fresh thyme sprigs.

Chermoula chicken and nutty couscous

This North African-style dish is a beautifully spicy way to serve chicken; the spices add so much flavour that it needs little salt.

SERVES 4
TAKES 15 MINUTES, 20–25 MINUTES
IN THE OVEN, PLUS MARINATING

8 chicken thighs, skin on,
  slashed with a knife
3 garlic cloves, crushed
2 tbsp olive oil
2 tbsp honey
Grated zest of 2 lemons
1½ tsp ground cumin
1 tsp hot paprika
½ tsp chilli powder
200g couscous
1 tbsp extra-virgin olive oil
300ml chicken stock, hot
3 tbsp chopped fresh flatleaf
  parsley
Juice of ½ lemon
25g toasted hazelnuts, chopped

1. Preheat the oven to 200°C/fan 180°C/gas 6. Marinate the chicken thighs in a bowl with the garlic, olive oil, honey, zest of 1 lemon, ground cumin, paprika and chilli powder. Mix together to coat the chicken, season and set aside for 15 minutes.

2. Put the chicken and marinade in a shallow roasting tin and roast for 20–25 minutes, until cooked through.

3. Meanwhile, in a bowl, mix the couscous with the remaining lemon zest and the extra-virgin olive oil, and pour over the hot chicken stock. Cover and leave for 10 minutes, then add the parsley, lemon juice and chopped hazelnuts. Mix with a fork and serve with the chicken.

Chicken tart with leeks and Gruyère

This dish is a great low-cost recipe for the whole family, and one that doesn't scrimp on taste.

SERVES 4
TAKES 10 MINUTES, 45–50 MINUTES IN THE OVEN, PLUS CHILLING

Flour, for dusting
500g pack shortcrust pastry
1 tbsp olive oil
Knob of butter, plus extra
  for greasing
2 large leeks, sliced
3 fresh thyme sprigs
2 tbsp wholegrain mustard
110g cooked chicken
3 large free-range eggs
284ml carton double cream
50g Gruyère, grated
Green salad, to serve

Variation Use bacon instead of chicken: just snip 5–6 rashers of back bacon into pieces and fry until crisp. Add to the tart case as in step 4.

1. Preheat the oven to 200°C/fan 180°C/gas 6. Roll out the shortcrust pastry on a lightly floured surface and press into a greased, 23cm-round loose-bottomed, fluted tart tin, allowing the pastry to drape slightly over the edges, then trim any excess. Prick the base all over with a fork and chill in the fridge for 10 minutes.

2. Line the pastry with kitchen foil and baking beans or rice and bake for 10 minutes. Remove the beans and foil, and return to the oven for a further 5 minutes, until the pastry is a pale biscuit colour.

3. Turn the oven temperature down to 180°C/fan 160°C/gas 4. Heat a frying pan with the olive oil and butter, and gently fry the leeks and thyme for 5 minutes, until tender. Spread the base of the tart with mustard, then top with the herby leek mixture.

4. Shred the cooked chicken and put in the tart case. Mix together the eggs, double cream and Gruyère. Season well with salt and pepper, and pour into the tart case. Bake for 25–30 minutes, until set and golden. Carefully remove from the tin. Serve with a green salad.

★DELICIOUS. TIP Don't waste the trimmings from your pastry – re-roll them, cut into small discs and place them in shallow tartlet tins. Add a dollop of jam and make delicious jam tarts for tea or pudding.

Chicken and broccoli stir-fry with wholewheat spaghetti

This healthy dish is a delicious mix of styles from different world cuisines.

SERVES **2**
READY IN **20** MINUTES

75g wholewheat spaghetti
1 tsp sunflower oil
2 skinless boneless chicken breasts, cut into thin strips
200g broccoli, cut into florets
1 tbsp soy sauce
2 tbsp sweet chilli sauce
100g beansprouts
1 mild red chilli, seeded and finely chopped
4 spring onions, thinly sliced
2 tsp sesame seeds, toasted

1. Cook the spaghetti in a pan of boiling water according to the packet instructions.

2. Meanwhile, heat the oil in a wok and stir-fry the chicken for 2 minutes, then add the broccoli and stir-fry for a further 2 minutes.

3. Mix together the soy sauce, sweet chilli sauce and 2 tablespoons of water. Add to the wok and, once bubbling, stir in the beansprouts and chilli. Cook for a minute or so until the beansprouts look a little translucent.

4. Drain the spaghetti and add to the pan with the spring onions and sesame seeds. Stir together and serve piping hot.

★DELICIOUS. TIP Unless you have a super-sized wok, never attempt a stir-fry for more than 2 people, as a large quantity of ingredients makes it difficult for the wok to maintain the high heat essential for good results. You can use Japanese wholewheat soba noodles (from oriental stores) instead of the wholewheat spaghetti, if you like.

Spicy crumbed chicken with coleslaw

Chicken drumsticks are good value, and this recipe beats fried chicken hands down – and it is much healthier too.

SERVES 4
TAKES 20 MINUTES, PLUS
25 MINUTES IN THE OVEN

30g packet fajita seasoning
2 tbsp plain flour
100g fresh white breadcrumbs
2 eggs
8 chicken drumsticks
3 tbsp vegetable oil

For the coleslaw
4 tbsp light mayonnaise
Juice of ½ lemon
350g white cabbage, cored and
  finely shredded
1 small red onion, finely sliced
1 medium carrot, coarsely
  grated

1. Preheat the oven to 200°C/fan 180°C/gas 6. Line a roasting tin with foil. Divide the fajita seasoning between 2 bowls, add the flour to 1 bowl and the breadcrumbs to the other. Stir to mix. Beat the eggs in a third bowl.

2. Toss the chicken in the flour. Dip each drumstick in the egg, then evenly in the breadcrumbs. Add to the tin, drizzle with the oil and bake for 25 minutes, turning halfway, until cooked, deep golden and crispy.

3. Meanwhile, make the coleslaw by mixing all the ingredients in a bowl. Season and serve with the chicken.

Creamy chicken cobbler

This delicious dish won't bust the budget and takes half an hour to cook. Turkey is an even cheaper alternative.

SERVES 4

TAKES 15 MINUTES, PLUS
15–20 MINUTES IN THE OVEN

1 tbsp olive oil
1 onion, finely chopped
1 leek, sliced and washed
2 garlic cloves, crushed
6 skinless boneless chicken
  thighs, sliced
2 tbsp fresh thyme leaves
1 tbsp plain flour
1 chicken stock cube
300g frozen peas
75ml double cream

For the cobbler
125g plain flour
1 tsp baking powder
1 small egg, beaten
75ml buttermilk

1. Preheat the oven to 220°C/fan 200°C/gas 7. Heat the oil in a large pan over a medium heat. Add the onion and leek, and gently fry for 5 minutes, until soft. Add the garlic and cook for a further minute. Add the chicken and thyme, and brown the chicken all over. Stir in the flour, cook for 30 seconds, then crumble the stock cube into 300ml boiling water, add to the pan and stir in the peas and cream. Season well.

2. In a bowl, mix together the cobbler ingredients and season. Pour the creamy chicken into 4 small (about 300ml) ovenproof dishes and dollop a tablespoon of the cobbler mixture on to the edge of each dish. Bake for 15–20 minutes, until cooked and the cobbler is risen and golden brown.

Variation As an alternative, follow the creamy chicken recipe but swap tarragon for the thyme. Spoon into a dish and top with mashed potato, then bake in the oven until golden and bubbling.

All-in-one baked lemon and rosemary chicken

Cheaper chicken cuts are baked with Mediterranean flavours to create a zingy summer supper.

SERVES 4
TAKES 10 MINUTES, PLUS
40–50 MINUTES IN THE OVEN

8 chicken portions (use legs, thighs and breasts)
500g new potatoes, halved lengthways
2 lemons, cut into wedges
4 fresh rosemary sprigs
1 glass of white wine
4 tbsp olive oil

1. Put the chicken portions into a roasting tin with the new potatoes, lemon wedges, fresh rosemary sprigs, white wine and olive oil, and season well.

2. Bake, uncovered, in a preheated oven at 180°C/fan 160°C/gas 4 for 40–50 minutes, until tender and golden.

Parmesan turkey escalopes

Turkey steaks are easy to flatten out for these crisp, pan-fried escalopes and they make a cheap but just as healthy alternative to fish.

SERVES 2
READY IN 20 MINUTES

2 turkey steaks
1 egg, beaten
3 tbsp grated Parmesan or
  Grana Padano
3 tbsp breadcrumbs
1 tbsp sunflower oil
Small knob of butter
1 tbsp finely chopped fresh
  rosemary
Chutney, boiled potatoes and
  salad, to serve

1. Using a rolling pin, flatten the turkey steaks between sheets of cling film. Season with salt and pepper, and dip into the beaten egg.

2. Mix the cheese and breadcrumbs together, and use to coat the turkey on both sides.

3. Heat the oil and butter in a frying pan, and when hot add the turkey and rosemary. Fry the turkey for 3–4 minutes on each side until golden and no longer pink in the centre.

4. Serve with chutney, boiled potatoes and salad.

Sticky harissa chicken thighs

You can serve this chicken dish with a crunchy dressed salad instead of the rice, if you like.

SERVES 2
READY IN 25 MINUTES

1 tbsp harissa paste
1 tbsp clear honey
6 skinless free-range chicken
  thighs
Oil, for greasing
350g pack ready-cooked Thai
  sticky rice
50g mangetout
4 spring onions, thinly sliced
  on the diagonal
Fresh coriander leaves,
  roughly chopped

1. Preheat the grill to high. Mix together the harissa with the honey. Lightly slash the chicken thighs and brush all over with the marinade.

2. Set aside for 10 minutes, then place the thighs on a lightly oiled baking sheet and pop under the grill for 12 minutes, turning halfway, until sticky and cooked through.

3. Meanwhile, heat the Thai sticky rice according to the packet instructions. Blanch the mangetout in boiling salted water for 2 minutes. Drain and halve the mangetout lengthways, then stir into the drained, cooked rice along with the spring onions and coriander leaves. Serve with the sticky chicken.

Biryani-style baked chicken and rice

A substantial and satisfying Indian-inspired meal that costs a fraction of a take-away.

SERVES 4

TAKES 20 MINUTES, PLUS ABOUT 30 MINUTES IN THE OVEN

2 tbsp olive oil
8 chicken thighs, bone in and skin on
1 large onion, finely chopped
3 garlic cloves, sliced
2 tsp garam masala
1 tsp ground ginger
1 green chilli, finely sliced
300g basmati rice
650ml chicken stock, hot
200g frozen mixed green vegetables
2 tbsp chopped fresh flatleaf parsley, to scatter

1. Preheat the oven to 190°C/fan 170°C/gas 5. Heat the oil in a large roasting tin on the hob. Add the chicken and fry over a high heat until golden brown all over. Remove from the tin and set aside.

2. Add the onion from the tin and cook gently for 6–8 minutes. Stir in the garlic, garam masala, ginger and chilli. Stir in the rice and cook for 1 minute. Top with the chicken and pour over the stock.

3. Cover with foil and bake for 20 minutes, until the rice has nearly absorbed all of the stock. Add a dash of hot water if the rice looks dry. Uncover and stir in the frozen vegetables. Re-cover and bake for 8–10 minutes, until everything is cooked. Scatter with parsley to serve.

Variation Use salmon fillets, skin on, instead of the chicken. Pan-fry briefly in step 1, then put on the rice in step 3, after the vegetables.

Sticky lime and ginger chicken

Low in fat but packed with flavour, this chicken recipe is deliciously sweet, sour and sticky and can easily be doubled to feed the family.

SERVES 2
TAKES 10 MINUTES, PLUS
25–30 MINUTES IN THE OVEN

3 globes stem ginger in syrup
2 tbsp honey
2 tbsp soy sauce
Finely grated zest of 2 limes,
  and juice of 1
2 garlic cloves, crushed
6 skinless chicken thighs
Steamed basmati rice and
  Tenderstem broccoli, to serve

1. Preheat the oven to 230°C/fan 210°C/gas 8. Drain and finely dice the ginger and mix with the honey, soy sauce, lime zest and juice and garlic cloves in a bowl.

2. Add the chicken thighs and mix together well. Spread out in a foil-lined or ceramic baking dish and bake for 25–30 minutes, turning over halfway, until cooked through.

3. Serve the chicken with steamed basmati rice and Tenderstem broccoli.

fish and
seafood

Spicy prawn and chickpea curry

Adding chickpeas is economical as you can use less expensive meat or fish. They are also really good for you.

SERVES 4
READY IN 35 MINUTES

2 tbsp olive oil
1 large red onion, sliced
1 garlic clove, sliced
1 tbsp harissa paste
400g can chopped tomatoes
½ tsp caster sugar
1 tsp red wine vinegar
400g can chickpeas, drained
  and rinsed
200g raw peeled king prawns
Handful of chopped fresh
  coriander
Good squeeze of fresh lime
  juice, plus lime wedges
  to garnish
Rice and flatbreads, to serve

1. Heat the olive oil in a pan over a low heat and fry the onion for 5 minutes until soft. Add the garlic and harissa paste, and cook for a further 2 minutes. Stir in the tomatoes, sugar and then vinegar, season and bring to a simmer.

2. Add the chickpeas. Simmer for 10 minutes, then stir in the prawns and cook for 3–4 minutes until they are pink.

3. Stir in the coriander and a good squeeze of lime juice, garnish with lime wedges, and serve with rice and flatbreads.

★DELICIOUS. TIP Try this with strips of cooked chicken breast instead of the king prawns.

Smoked haddock and sweetcorn chowder

A thick chowder that's quick and easy to make for four hungry mouths.

SERVES 4
READY IN 35 MINUTES

Small knob of butter
1 large onion, finely chopped
1 celery stick, finely chopped
1 leek, washed and finely chopped
3 medium potatoes, diced
600ml milk
200ml chicken or fish stock, hot
500g skinless smoked haddock, cut into 4cm pieces
326g can sweetcorn, drained and rinsed
Fresh flatleaf parsley, finely chopped, to garnish

1. Melt the butter in a large saucepan over a gentle heat. Add the chopped onion, celery and leek, and cook for 8–10 minutes, until softened.

2. Stir in the potatoes and toss with the vegetables. Pour over 400ml of the milk and top up with the stock. Bring to the boil, then reduce to a simmer for 15 minutes, until the potatoes are tender.

3. Meanwhile, put the fish and remaining milk in a separate pan and bring to the boil. Drain the liquid into the chowder. Set aside the fish.

4. Stir the sweetcorn into the chowder and heat for 1 minute. Remove from the heat, ladle half of the mixture into a food processor and whiz until smooth. Return to the pan and put over a gentle heat. Flake in the fish.

5. Gently heat the chowder until hot and ladle into bowls. Garnish with parsley and serve immediately.

Variation Replace the haddock with 1kg prepared live mussels. Add them in step 3 and cook for 4–5 minutes, then discard any that haven't opened. Remove the cooked mussels from the shells and return to the chowder at the end of step 4.

Fish fingers with chipped potatoes and tartare sauce

This is a great, cheap recipe to feed the family. Use ready-made tartare sauce if you don't have capers in your cupboard.

SERVES 4

TAKES 25 MINUTES, PLUS
45 MINUTES IN THE OVEN

1kg floury potatoes
3 tbsp vegetable oil, plus extra
  for frying
Large pinch of sea salt
150g plain flour, seasoned
2 eggs, beaten
100g fresh breadcrumbs
3 tbsp chopped fresh dill
700g sustainably caught white
  fish fillets
6 tbsp mayonnaise
1 tbsp capers, rinsed and
  chopped
Grated zest of 1 lemon, then
  cut into wedges to serve
  (optional)

1. Preheat the oven to 200°C/fan 180°C/gas 6. Cut the potatoes into cubes, put in a pan of simmering salted water, and cook for 2–3 minutes, until parboiled.

2. Drain, shake well and mix with the vegetable oil and some sea salt in a roasting tin. Roast for 45 minutes, until golden and very crispy.

3. Meanwhile, put the plain flour in a dish. Place the eggs in another dish and the breadcrumbs, mixed with 2 tablespoons of the dill, in a third.

4. Cut the white fish fillets into fingers and dip each into the flour, egg and breadcrumbs in turn and place on a non-stick baking sheet.

5. Mix the mayonnaise in a bowl with the capers, lemon zest and remaining dill. Season and chill.

6. Heat a good layer of vegetable oil in a pan and fry the fish fingers for 2–3 minutes on each side, until golden and cooked through. Serve with the potatoes, sauce and lemon wedges, if you like.

Tuna Niçoise pasta

The classic Mediterranean salad is given a makeover using pasta. Using tinned tuna makes it more affordable, too.

SERVES 4
READY IN 30 MINUTES

300g pappardelle or pasta shapes
100g green beans, trimmed
2 tbsp extra-virgin olive oil
3 tbsp olive oil
2 shallots, finely sliced
3 anchovy fillets, chopped
1 tbsp capers, rinsed
Handful of pitted black olives, halved
14 cherry tomatoes, halved
Juice of ½ lemon
2 x 200g cans tuna
Handful of chopped fresh parsley
Hard-boiled eggs, peeled and halved, to serve (optional)

1. Cook the pappardelle or pasta shapes in a saucepan of boiling salted water according to the packet instructions. When the pasta has a few minutes left, add the green beans and cook until both are al dente.

2. Drain, reserving 2 tablespoons of the cooking water. In a bowl, mix the pasta and beans with the extra-virgin olive oil and the cooking water.

3. Meanwhile, heat the olive oil in a small frying pan over a medium heat and gently fry the shallots for 5 minutes.

4. Add the anchovy fillets, capers, pitted black olives and cherry tomatoes. Warm for 3–4 minutes, then remove from the heat and stir in the lemon juice.

5. Drain the tuna, flake and stir into the pasta with the sauce and the parsley. Divide among 4 bowls and garnish with hard-boiled eggs, if using.

Crunchy fish burgers

These burgers have a real kick to them. For a milder flavour, mix some mayonnaise with a little Dijon mustard and spread on the fish before rolling in the polenta.

SERVES 4
READY IN 20 MINUTES

4 x 150g pieces sustainably caught skinless white fish, such as pollack, haddock or large whiting
2 tbsp curry paste, mixed with 1 tbsp olive oil
175g polenta
2 spring onions, very finely chopped
Juice and zest of 1 lemon
Vegetable oil, for shallow frying
4 soft bread rolls or sliced crusty white bread
Mayonnaise, salad leaves, cress, cucumber slices, lime pickle, to fill
Lime wedges, to serve

1. Dry the fish on kitchen paper, then smear all over with the curry paste. Mix the polenta on a plate with the spring onions, lemon juice and zest. Press the fish into the polenta to cover.

2. Heat the oil in a frying pan and cook the fish for 3–4 minutes each side, until golden and cooked through. Drain on kitchen paper.

3. Spread the rolls or bread with a little mayonnaise. Sandwich around the salad leaves, cress, fish, cucumber and pickle. Serve with lime wedges.

Variation Cut the fish into thick fingers before coating in polenta and frying. Serve with potato wedges and peas.

Baked fish with a herb and lemon crust

Quick, light and easy, this healthy fish supper can leave you feeling virtuous – and not just because of the price.

SERVES 4

TAKES 15 MINUTES, PLUS
10–12 MINUTES IN THE OVEN

1 tbsp extra-virgin olive oil, plus extra for greasing
4 x 175g skinned thick white fish fillets, such as hake, haddock or sustainably caught cod
4 slices white bread, toasted and crusts removed
1 garlic clove, crushed
Finely grated zest of 1 small lemon, plus 1 tsp lemon juice
15g each fresh tarragon, fresh chives and fresh flatleaf parsley, mixed
4 tbsp extra-light mayonnaise
3 tbsp natural yogurt
½ tsp Dijon mustard
4 cocktail gherkins, finely chopped
1 tbsp capers, drained and finely chopped

1. Preheat the oven to 230°C/fan 210°C/gas 8. Line a baking sheet with baking parchment and lightly grease with oil. Season the fish all over and put, skinned-side down, on the paper.

2. Break the toast into a food processor, add the garlic and lemon zest, and whiz into fine crumbs. Add 25g of the mixed fresh herbs and whiz again, until the herbs are finely chopped. Add the lemon juice and oil, season and whiz briefly to mix.

3. Carefully press the breadcrumb mixture on to each piece of fish. Slide the sheet on to the top shelf of the oven and bake for 10–12 minutes or until the topping is golden and the fish is opaque and cooked through.

4. Meanwhile, make the tartare sauce. Chop the remaining herbs (reserve a few chives to garnish the sauce) and mix with the mayonnaise, yogurt, mustard, gherkins, capers and a little salt. Serve the fish on warmed plates with the tartare sauce.

Salmon and potato bake

What's not to like about this salmon dish? It's a filling, budget-friendly recipe that will feed four generously.

SERVES 4
TAKES 20 MINUTES, PLUS
20–30 MINUTES IN THE OVEN

1kg floury potatoes, cut into
  3mm slices
1 tbsp olive oil
1 large red onion, sliced
1 tbsp plain flour
Few handfuls of baby leaf
  spinach
Butter, for greasing
3 skinless salmon fillets, sliced
200ml double cream
50g grated Gruyère

1. Preheat the oven to 180°C/fan 160°C/gas 4. Bring a pan of salted water to the boil, then simmer the potatoes for 2–3 minutes. Drain and set aside.

2. Heat the olive oil in a frying pan and gently fry the red onion for 5 minutes, then stir in the plain flour and season well.

3. Wilt a few handfuls of baby spinach in a pan over a medium heat, then squeeze out the excess liquid. Butter a 1.2-litre ovenproof dish and layer up the potatoes and onion with the salmon fillets and the spinach, finishing with a layer of potato.

4. Pour the double cream over the top. Sprinkle with the Gruyère and bake for 20–30 minutes, until golden and bubbling.

Roasted salmon with simple white wine and thyme risotto

This satisfying bowl makes a smart yet surprisingly economical dinner-party dish.

SERVES 4
TAKES 25 MINUTES, PLUS
10–12 MINUTES IN THE OVEN

600g piece skinless boneless salmon fillet
½ tsp sea salt
Grated zest and juice of 1 lemon
1 tbsp olive oil
Small knob of butter
1 large onion, chopped
2 garlic cloves, chopped
4 fresh thyme sprigs
400g carnaroli or arborio risotto rice
250ml dry white wine, ideally Italian
1 litre fresh chicken stock, hot

1. Preheat the oven to 220°C/fan 200°C/gas 7. Place the salmon on a baking sheet, sprinkle with the sea salt and lemon zest. Pour over the lemon juice and leave for 5 minutes. Roast for 10–12 minutes or until golden and just cooked through. Set aside to rest.

2. Meanwhile, heat the olive oil and butter in a large frying pan over a medium heat. Add the onion, garlic and thyme, and cook, stirring occasionally, for 5 minutes, until the onion has softened.

3. Stir in the rice and cook for 1 minute. Add the wine and boil vigorously for 2–3 minutes, until evaporated. Pour in the stock, a third at a time, adding more when the last is absorbed, and simmer gently for 15 minutes, stirring regularly, until all the liquid has evaporated and the rice is creamy and just tender.

4. Divide the risotto among bowls and flake the salmon over the top. Grind over plenty of black pepper and serve.

Spicy sweet potato fishcakes

The sweet potatoes in these fishcakes add a new depth of flavour. If you don't have polenta, roll the fishcakes in fine breadcrumbs.

SERVES 4 (MAKES 8)
TAKES 40 MINUTES

2 sweet potatoes, cut into chunks
250g potatoes, cut into chunks
500g skinless white fish fillets
1 red chilli, seeded and finely chopped
2 tbsp chopped fresh coriander
100g polenta
4 tbsp vegetable oil
Crunchy salad, to serve

1. Place all the potatoes in a pan of cold salted water. Bring to the boil and simmer for 15 minutes, until tender. Drain, mash and set aside to cool.

2. Meanwhile, put the fish fillets in a saucepan and cover with cold water. Bring to the boil, then turn off the heat and leave to cook for 6–8 minutes.

3. Remove the fish fillets from the water, drain and flake into the mashed potato. Stir the chilli and coriander into the mixture, then adjust the seasoning to taste.

4. Shape the mixture into 8 balls, flatten them slightly and chill until ready to cook.

5. Place the polenta on a plate and roll the fishcakes in it, to coat. Heat the oil in a pan and fry the fishcakes for 4–5 minutes each side, until golden and piping hot.

6. Serve with a crunchy salad.

★DELICIOUS. TIP For fishcakes you can forgo expensive cod or haddock and use less well-known, more affordable fish, such as pollack or coley. Check out the Marine Stewardship Council's website, www.msc.org, for a list of good sustainable fish to eat.

Teriyaki salmon with stir-fry vegetables

This Asian dish is smart enough to serve for a dinner for four, yet cheap enough to make midweek.

SERVES 4
TAKES 20 MINUTES

4 tbsp teriyaki sauce
2 tbsp sweet chilli sauce
Grated zest of 1 lime and a
  squeeze of juice
4 salmon fillets
1 tbsp vegetable oil
300g pack stir-fry vegetables
2 tbsp soy sauce
Sesame oil, to drizzle

1. Mix the teriyaki sauce, sweet chilli sauce and lime zest and juice in a large bowl. Add the salmon fillets and turn to coat, then marinate for 15 minutes.

2. Heat the vegetable oil in a large frying pan and add the salmon fillets, reserving the marinade. Fry ths salmon for 4–5 minutes each side, until slightly blackened. Set aside.

3. Add the reserved marinade to the pan and reduce slightly. Cook the pack of stir-fry vegetables in another pan with a splash of water and the soy sauce for 2–3 minutes.

4. Divide the stir-fry vegetables among 4 plates, top each portion of vegetables with a salmon fillet and drizzle with the reduced marinade. Drizzle with a little sesame oil and serve.

★DELICIOUS. TIP Look out for supermarket offers or buy a larger tail-end piece of salmon from the fish counter and cut it into steaks yourself. Try to buy sustainably farmed fish, or fish that meets the standards of the Marine Stewardship Council (MSC), which helps to protect fish stocks.

Smoked mackerel and couscous salad

Try a taste of North Africa with this zesty fish and couscous salad, made with cucumber and dried apricots.

SERVES 4
READY IN 15 MINUTES

200g couscous
150g broccoli, cut into small florets
Grated zest and juice of ½ lemon, plus extra wedges to serve
1 tbsp extra-virgin olive oil
¼ cucumber, halved lengthways, seeded and diced
100g dried ready-to-eat apricots, roughly chopped
200g peppered smoked mackerel fillets, skinned and flaked
15g pumpkin seeds
15g sunflower seeds
50g blanched whole almonds, toasted, to serve (optional)

1. Put the couscous in a large bowl and pour over 250ml boiling water. Cover and leave for 5 minutes, until the liquid has been absorbed. Fluff up the grains with a fork. Set aside.

2. Meanwhile, blanch the broccoli in boiling water for 3 minutes, until just tender. Drain, plunge into cold water, then drain again and pat dry on kitchen paper. Set aside.

3. In a small bowl, mix together the lemon zest and juice with the oil. Pour over the couscous, season well and toss together. Add the cucumber, apricots and broccoli, and toss again. Divide among 4 plates, top with the mackerel and seeds, and serve with the lemon wedges and the almonds, if you like.

Variation Use char-grilled chicken instead of mackerel, and vary the vegetables too. Add peas, dried cranberries or raisins and walnuts, if you prefer.

Vegetable biryani

The spicy flavours in this dish will really get your tastebuds racing and make you a winner in the budget stakes.

SERVES 4
READY IN 30 MINUTES

3 tbsp groundnut or vegetable oil
2 tsp grated fresh ginger
2 garlic cloves, crushed
1 green chilli, seeded and sliced
2 tbsp biryani curry paste
500g chopped mixed vegetables
   (such as cauliflower, sweet
   potato and green beans)
2 tomatoes, seeded and chopped
3 shallots, finely sliced
400g natural yogurt
Basmati rice, to serve

1. Heat 2 tablespoons of the groundnut or vegetable oil in a pan and gently fry the ginger, garlic and chilli for a couple of minutes.

2. Add the biryani paste and cook for 1 minute, then add the chopped mixed vegetables, tomatoes and a good splash of water, and cook for 10–12 minutes.

3. Meanwhile, heat the remaining oil in a pan and fry the shallots until crispy.

4. Season the curry, add the yogurt and simmer for a further 5 minutes. Sprinkle the curry with the crispy shallots before serving with basmati rice.

★DELICIOUS. TIP Jazz up some basmati rice to go with the curry by mixing in some toasted cashew nuts and juicy sultanas just before serving.

Roast vegetable and houmous pie

The sweet potato in this vegetarian-pie base absorbs the steam released from the baking vegetables, keeping the pastry crisp.

SERVES 4

TAKES 15 MINUTES, PLUS 1 HOUR IN THE OVEN

1 onion, cut into wedges
50g small broccoli florets
1 each red and yellow peppers, seeded and cut into chunks
2 courgettes, thickly sliced
2 tsp cumin seeds
1 tbsp olive oil
200g houmous
Finely grated zest of 1 lemon
2 tbsp chopped fresh coriander
375g pack ready-rolled puff pastry
2 small sweet potatoes, thinly sliced
1 egg yolk, mixed with 1 tbsp milk, for glazing
Dressed mixed salad, to serve

1. Preheat the oven to 220°C/fan 200°C/gas 7. Mix the onion, broccoli, peppers and courgettes in a roasting tin, tossing well with the cumin seeds and the oil. Roast for 30 minutes.

2. Remove from the oven and mix in the houmous, lemon zest and coriander. Turn the oven down to 200°C/fan 180°C/gas 6. Cut the pastry in half to make 2 squares. Transfer 1 piece to a lined baking sheet and arrange the sweet potato slices in slightly overlapping layers to cover the pastry, leaving a 2cm border. Pile the roasted veg on top of the potatoes and brush the border with the egg glaze.

3. Roll the remaining pastry out a little thinner. Drape over the filling, press the pastry edges together to seal and trim away any excess pastry. Egg wash the top and cut 3 diagonal slits in the pastry.

4. Bake for 25–30 minutes, until the pastry is golden brown and puffed up. Serve with a dressed mixed salad.

★DELICIOUS. TIP Substitute the broccoli for cauliflower florets. Freeze at the end of step 3 for up to 3 months. Thaw then bake for 30–35 minutes.

Pearl barley risotto with roasted squash, red peppers and rocket

A vegetarian risotto made with pearl barley instead of the usual rice makes a tasty and wallet-conscious winter meal.

SERVES 4

TAKES 45 MINUTES, PLUS 35 MINUTES IN THE OVEN

- 450g peeled butternut squash, cut into 2cm chunks
- 2 red peppers, halved, seeded and cut into chunky pieces
- 2 tbsp extra-virgin olive oil
- 1 medium onion, finely chopped
- 2 garlic cloves, finely chopped
- Leaves from 3 large fresh thyme sprigs
- 350g pearl barley
- 1.5 litres vegetable stock, hot
- 3 tbsp chopped fresh flatleaf parsley
- 4 small handfuls of rocket or spinach and vegetarian Parmesan shavings, to garnish

1. Preheat the oven to 200°C/fan 180°C/gas 6. Put the squash and peppers in a small roasting tin, drizzle with 1 tablespoon of the oil, season and toss. Roast for 35 minutes or until tender, turning halfway, then remove from the oven and set aside.

2. Meanwhile, start the risotto. Heat the remaining oil in a medium pan over a medium–low heat. Add the onion, garlic and thyme leaves, and cook gently, stirring occasionally, for 6–8 minutes, until softened. Add the pearl barley and cook for 1 minute.

3. Add a quarter of the stock to the pan and simmer, stirring occasionally, until all the stock has been absorbed. Add another quarter of the stock and continue in this way until all the stock is absorbed – it should take about 40 minutes for the barley to be tender but still al dente.

4. Stir in the parsley followed by the squash and peppers. Season and spoon into warmed bowls. Serve topped with the rocket or spinach and some Parmesan shavings.

Crunchy Thai-style tofu and peanut salad

A healthy, satisfying vegetarian salad for two that comes with a kick you can afford.

SERVES 2
READY IN 25 MINUTES

250g pack tofu
4 tbsp Thai sweet chilli dipping sauce
1 tbsp dark soy sauce, plus extra to drizzle
1 tbsp toasted sesame oil
300g pack vegetable and beansprout stir-fry
25g dry-roasted peanuts, roughly chopped, plus extra to sprinkle

1. Drain the tofu, pat dry with kitchen paper and cut into chunky bite-sized pieces. Put into a bowl, add 2 tablespoons of Thai sweet chilli dipping sauce and the dark soy sauce. Toss together and set aside to marinate for 15 minutes.

2. Heat the toasted sesame oil in a wok or large frying pan over a medium–high heat. When hot, add the tofu and cook for 3–4 minutes, turning halfway, until golden and sticky. Set aside in a large bowl to cool slightly.

3. Add the vegetables and beansprouts, the roasted peanuts and the remaining 2 tablespoons of Thai sweet chilli dipping sauce to the wok or frying pan and toss together well. Cook for a further minute.

4. Divide between 2 wide bowls and scatter with extra roasted peanuts. Serve with extra dark soy sauce to drizzle over.

Spicy stuffed butternut squash

This colourful, cheesy vegetarian dish looks great and is satisfyingly filling too.

SERVES 4
TAKES 25 MINUTES AND
20–25 MINUTES IN THE OVEN

2 butternut squash, halved
  lengthways and seeded
2 tbsp olive oil
1 red chilli, seeded and finely
  chopped
300g bag baby leaf spinach
Juice of ½ lemon
100g goat's cheese, crumbled
2 tbsp pumpkin seeds

1. Preheat the oven to 180°C/fan 160°C/gas 4. Cut off the long halves of each squash and put the round halves on a baking sheet. Drizzle with 1 tablespoon of oil and roast for 20–25 minutes.

2. Meanwhile, peel the remaining squash and cut into cubes. Heat the remaining oil in a frying pan and fry the cubed squash with the chilli for 5–10 minutes, until tender. Stir in the spinach until wilted and season well.

3. Remove from the heat and stir in the lemon juice, cheese and pumpkin seeds. Remove the squash from the oven and heat the grill to medium.
Fill the squash halves with the spinach mixture and grill for 5 minutes, until the cheese has melted.

Variation Instead of stuffing the squash, peel and cube it all, then pan-fry as in step 2. Stir in the spinach, lemon juice, goat's cheese and pumpkin seeds, as in step 3, then stir through cooked pasta.

Potato and Stilton soup

This is a lovely, warming winter broth that makes a filling yet frugal lunchtime meal.

SERVES 6–8
READY IN 50 MINUTES

Large knob of butter
2 onions, chopped
2 celery sticks, chopped
2 fresh thyme sprigs
1kg Maris Piper potatoes, diced
2 litres chicken or vegetable
  stock, hot
200g Stilton, crumbled
142ml double cream
Scones or crusty bread, to serve

1. Heat the butter in a large saucepan, add the onions and celery and cook for 10 minutes, until nicely softened.

2. Add the thyme, potatoes and stock, and bring to the boil. Simmer gently for 30 minutes, until the potatoes fall apart when poked with a knife. Lift out the thyme stalks and discard. Using a hand-held blender, whiz the soup until smooth.

3. Stir in most of the cheese and all of the cream, and heat through gently. Ladle into bowls, grind over black pepper, sprinkle over the remaining cheese and serve with scones or crusty bread.

Potato, Cheshire cheese and spring onion tarts

These tarts are really easy to make and filling enough to serve as a main course. They also look really impressive.

SERVES 4

TAKES 20 MINUTES, PLUS
25–30 MINUTES IN THE OVEN

3 large (about 700g) white
  potatoes
500g block of puff pastry,
  thawed if frozen
Flour, for dusting
6 tbsp extra-thick double cream
100g Cheshire cheese, crumbled
1 bunch spring onions, finely
  sliced
Mixed green salad, to serve

1. Peel the potatoes and cut into 3mm-thick slices. Cook in a pan of boiling salted water for 4 minutes or until just tender but still holding their shape. Drain carefully so they don't break up, then set aside to cool and dry on a clean tea towel.

2. Meanwhile, preheat the oven to 200°C/fan 180°C/gas 6. Roll out the pastry on a lightly floured surface to about 36cm square. Using a 16cm or so plate or bowl as a template, cut out 4 pastry circles and pop on to 2 large non-stick baking sheets. Discard the pastry trimmings.

3. Arrange half the potatoes on the pastry circles, leaving a small border all around. Spread the potatoes with half the cream, then season and crumble over half the cheese. Top with nearly all the onions (save the rest for garnish) and the remaining potatoes. Sprinkle with the remaining cheese, then place a small dollop of the rest of the cream in the centre of each. Season with black pepper only.

4. Bake the tarts for 25–30 minutes, swapping the sheets over halfway, until the pastry is cooked and golden and the topping is melting. Cool on the sheets for about 5 minutes, then transfer each tart to a serving plate. Top with the reserved spring onions to garnish. Serve with a mixed green salad.

Variation For non-vegetarians, add diced pancetta to the tarts just before baking. Both versions taste as good served cold as hot.

Spinach and egg pizza

Bored with conventional pizzas? Try this delicious spinach and egg version.

SERVES 4
TAKES ABOUT 35 MINUTES,
20 MINUTES IN THE OVEN,
PLUS PROVING

1 tbsp olive oil, plus extra for
  greasing
1 large onion, finely chopped
2 tbsp tomato purée
1 tbsp mixed dried herbs
400g can plum tomatoes
225g fresh spinach, washed
2 x 150g balls mozzarella,
  chopped
4 medium eggs
Green salad, to serve

For the dough
350g strong plain bread flour,
  plus extra for dusting
¾ tsp fine salt
¾ tsp fast-action dried yeast
1 tbsp olive oil

1. Make the dough. Sift the flour and salt into a bowl. Stir in the yeast, then gradually mix in 200ml tepid water and the oil, to form a soft dough. Knead on a lightly floured surface for 5 minutes. Put into an oiled bowl, cover and set aside for 1 hour, until doubled in size.

2. Meanwhile, heat the oil in a frying pan over a medium heat. Cook the onion for 5 minutes, until softened. Stir in the tomato purée and herbs, cook for 1 minute, then add the tomatoes, breaking them up with a spoon. Simmer for 15 minutes, until thickened. Season and set aside.

3. Preheat the oven to 230°C/fan 210°C/gas 8. Knead the dough again, then roll out to a large, thin rectangle. Press on to a large, oiled baking sheet and spread with the tomato sauce. Put the spinach in a colander, pour over boiling water and squeeze out the liquid. Scatter the wilted spinach over the pizza, top with the cheese and season. Bake for 15 minutes.

4. Crack the eggs onto the pizza and return to the oven for 5 minutes, until just set. Serve with a green salad.

Variation Ring the changes by adding different toppings such as strips of ham or Parma ham, sliced mushrooms, red peppers, pepperoni or chorizo and plenty of grated Cheddar cheese.

Stilton and leek bread and butter bake

A cost-conscious cheesy take on a classic British dish.

SERVES 4

TAKES 15 MINUTES, 30–40 MINUTES
IN THE OVEN, PLUS SOAKING

30g butter, plus extra for
  greasing
2 large leeks, trimmed,
  washed and cut into medium
  slices
1 tbsp Dijon mustard
8 medium slices granary bread
3 eggs
500ml whole milk
200g Stilton, crumbled
200g Cheddar, grated
Steamed seasonal vegetables,
  to serve

1. Heat 10g of the butter in a large frying pan over a medium–low heat. Add the leeks and cook gently for 6–8 minutes, stirring occasionally, until softened but not coloured. Set aside.

2. Preheat the oven to 190°C/fan 170°C/gas 5. Meanwhile, thinly spread the remaining butter and the mustard on 1 side of each slice of bread. Cut each slice into quarters. In a large jug, beat together the eggs, milk and some seasoning.

3. Arrange a third of the bread, buttered-side up, in a buttered ovenproof dish. Scatter with a third of the leeks and a third of each cheese, then pour over a third of the milk mixture, evenly and slowly. Repeat to use up the remaining ingredients, then leave to soak for 20 minutes or so, if you have time.

4. Place the dish on a baking sheet and cook for 30–40 minutes, until risen and golden. Serve warm with steamed seasonal vegetables.

Variation For a meaty version, fry 6 chopped pork sausages until golden, then add to the leeks before layering up.

desserts

Nutella mousse

Possibly the fastest and cheapest mousse you'll ever make.

SERVES 4

TAKES 5 MINUTES, PLUS CHILLING

250g Nutella
175g Greek yogurt or fromage
  frais
1 tsp espresso powder, blended
  with a little hot water
2 tbsp chopped toasted
  hazelnuts
Little biscuits, for dipping
Wedges of pear and halved
  hazelnuts, to decorate

1. Mix the Nutella with the Greek yogurt or fromage frais, the watered-down espresso powder, and the chopped toasted hazelnuts. Spoon into 4 little pots or ramekins and chill.

2. Serve with little shortbread biscuits for dipping, topped with wedges of pear and halved hazelnuts, if you like.

French toast

Satisfy your sweet tooth and your budget with luscious French toast, ready in just 10 minutes!

SERVES 6
READY IN **10** MINUTES

**6 thick slices brioche or
  panettone**
2 large eggs
2 tbsp milk
**3 tbsp sweet sherry or 1 tsp
  vanilla extract**
1 tsp caster sugar
Knob of butter, for frying
**Canned fruit, such as apricot
  halves, and ice cream,
  to serve**

1. Whisk the egg, milk and sweet sherry or vanilla extract in a shallow bowl. Add the brioche or panettone to the bowl to soak for 5 minutes.

2. Remove the soaked brioche or panettone from the mixture and dust each side with caster sugar, then pan-fry in a knob of butter until golden and caramelised.

3. Serve with canned fruit and ice cream.

Toffee apple trifle

This delectable trifle is made using storecupboard and fridge staples.

SERVES 6

TAKES 20 MINUTES, PLUS COOLING

2 Bramley apples, peeled, cored and chopped
70g caster sugar
Squeeze of fresh lemon juice
6 tbsp toffee sauce, such as dulce de leche
6 shortbread biscuits
150ml whipping cream
1 tbsp icing sugar
Toasted almonds, to decorate

1. Put the apples in a saucepan with the caster sugar and lemon juice. Cook for 10 minutes until really soft, then blitz in a food processor or mash with a fork until smooth. Cool.

2. Swirl through the toffee sauce. Divide among 6 individual glass bowls and crumble the shortbread biscuits over.

3. Whip the cream and sweeten it with the icing sugar. Spoon the sweet cream onto the crumbs. Top with toasted almonds and serve.

Warm chocolate croissants with ice cream

The best desserts are sumptuous, decadent and involve hardly any cooking. This one is exactly that.

SERVES 4
READY IN UNDER 10 MINUTES

1 x 100g bar plain or milk chocolate (according to your preference)
4 good-quality fresh croissants
Icing sugar, to dust
Vanilla ice cream and a handful of strawberries, to serve

1. Preheat the oven to 180°C/fan 160°C/gas 4. Break the chocolate into small squares.

2. Split open the croissants and tuck a few squares of chocolate into each one. Warm them through on a baking sheet in the oven for 5 minutes until the chocolate melts.

3. Dust the croissants with icing sugar, and serve with scoops of vanilla ice cream and a few strawberries on the side.

Pear and banana granola crumble

A variation on a traditional fruit crumble, this pud has storecupboard granola as the topping.

MAKES 4
TAKES 5 MINUTES, PLUS
15–20 MINUTES IN THE OVEN

1 banana, peeled and sliced
2 pears, peeled, cored and
  sliced
Handful of blueberries
2 tbsp fresh orange juice
75g granola
25g cold butter, diced
Cream or ice cream, to serve

1. Preheat the oven to 180°C/fan 160°C/gas 4. Divide the banana, pears and blueberries among 4 x 150ml ramekins and drizzle over the fresh orange juice.

2. Put the granola and butter in a separate bowl. Use your fingers to rub the butter lightly into the granola. Sprinkle the topping over the ramekins and bake for 15–20 minutes. Rest for 5 minutes, then serve with cream or ice cream.

Rhubarb and custard crumbles

Ever so easy and ever so delicious, you can rustle up this economical dessert in half an hour.

SERVES 4

TAKES 10 MINUTES, PLUS
15–20 MINUTES IN THE OVEN

50g butter, cubed, plus extra
  for greasing
400g forced pink rhubarb
1–2 stem ginger in syrup
  50g caster sugar, plus extra
  4 tsp
300ml ready-made fresh
  custard
75g plain flour
3 tbsp chopped toasted
  hazelnuts

1. Preheat the oven to 180°C/fan 160°C/gas 4. Butter 4 x 300ml ramekins or ovenproof dishes.

2. Cut the rhubarb into 2.5cm pieces and place in the bottom of the ramekins or dishes. Finely chop the stem ginger and add to the rhubarb with a little of the syrup from the jar. Sprinkle the 4 teaspoons of sugar over the rhubarb.

3. Divide the custard among the dishes and set aside.

4. Place the flour and butter in a bowl, and rub together until it resembles breadcrumbs. Stir in the 50g caster sugar and toasted hazelnuts then sprinkle over the rhubarb. Bake for 15–20 minutes until bubbling and golden.

Variation This recipe works well with any quick-cooking fruit – try cooking either apples, cut fairly small, halved apricots, plums or gooseberries.

Honey-nut bananas

Delicious and super speedy, this dessert is boozy and sexy
enough to share with friends. Omit the rum and it makes a great
cut-price family pud too.

SERVES 4
READY IN 8–10 MINUTES

40g butter
3–4 tbsp honey
4 bananas
Splash of rum
Chopped pecan nuts
Ice cream, to serve

1. Melt the butter with the honey in a heavy-based
frying pan and cook until just beginning to brown.

2. Slice the bananas in half lengthways and place
in the pan. Cook for 3–4 minutes, turning
occasionally, until caramelised.

3. Add a good splash of rum to the pan and allow to
evaporate (or light with a match and flambé, if you
like) then sprinkle with a few chopped pecans and
serve with ice cream.

Variation Make this with slices of fresh
peeled and cored pineapple too. The
rum is delicious, but you could use lime
juice instead for a non-alcoholic version.

Additional tips

Savvy shopping tips

There are loads of clever tricks you can employ to keep the price of your shopping down, and yet this doesn't mean scrimping and cutting back on treats!

• The best way to keep food bills low is to plan your weekly menu and make a shopping list accordingly, then stick to it as you go round and do not be tempted to buy what you don't need.

• Don't go shopping when you're hungry! Sounds obvious, but you are far more likely to buy more food when you're famished.

• Experiment with budget and own-label ranges, and compare prices and quality with the big brands.

• Stock up on non-perishable goods whenever you see them on offer, but be careful of bulk buying treats – they will get eaten just because they're there!

• Every now and again, have a no-shopping weekend where you live off what you've got in the storecupboard, fridge and freezer.

• Check out www.mysupermaket.co.uk, a website that helps you decide where to get the best price for your weekly shop.

• Shop online and you'll end up being less tempted by foods you didn't intend to buy.

• Buy from local farm shops or markets where fruit and vegetables are often a lot cheaper. Get to know your local independent retailers, as they will tell you what's good value each week and sometimes give you a little extra now and then in return for your loyalty.

• Make use of supermarket loyalty cards wherever possible and stack up points you can redeem against your shopping or other treats or activities.

How to avoid waste

Plan, plan, plan! The best way to keep your food bills down is to plan your weekly menu and make a shopping list. Don't be tempted to buy special offers unless you're sure you'll use everything.

FRUIT

● Buy loose rather than prepacked fruit and vegetables .

● Take advantage of buy one, get one free offers (BOGOFs) if you know you can consume all the produce or can freeze some of it.

● Remember that you can store citrus fruit, apples and pears longer in the fridge, so only put a few in the fruit bowl at a time. That way there's always fruit to tempt you, but not going soft and wrinkly in the heat of the room. When oranges, satsumas, lemons or limes have gone hard in the bottom of your fruit bowl, don't just throw them away; squeeze the juice and drink it, or slice the fruit and freeze it ready to pop into a glass of water or your gin and tonic.

● When pears are overripe there's not a lot you can do with them as they turn sweet and mushy, but at least peel, core and throw them into the liquidiser with apple or orange juice to make a fruit smoothie.

● Apples that are past their best are ideal for chopping up and adding to a cake mixture, or for pan-frying in butter and sugar to serve with pancakes or Madeira cake (add a splash of cream to the butter and sugar, and you'll have a creamy toffee sauce). Or when you've pan-fried sausages, pork chops or chicken breasts, add a few apple slices and sage leaves to the pan, and fry until golden and tender to serve with the meat.

BANANAS

Bananas are delicious when they are slightly browned and sweet, but many children won't eat them like this. Before they get too brown, peel the bananas, chop them, wrap in cling film and freeze. Place in a food processor with Greek yogurt and honey, and blend until smooth to make instant ice cream. This also works with frozen berries and frozen pineapple (peel and cut into smallish chunks). Blackened bananas make the best-ever cakes or muffins. Another delicious treat is mashed banana sandwiches with a layer of peanut butter and perhaps a rasher of bacon added as well. Naughty but nice!

SALAD

If you constantly throw away bags of salad leaves, buy whole lettuce instead; they will keep far longer in the salad drawer of the fridge. Or, if you've got space on the windowsill or on the patio, why not grow spinach or rocket in a windowbox or tub in the garden. Both are one of the easiest crops to grow, and you need only reach out to crop it fresh whenever you need it; these cut-and-come-again lettuce varieties will keep going for months.

LEFTOVER VEGETABLES

If at the end of the week the salad box in the bottom of your fridge contains half a cauliflower, a few broccoli stems, half a butternut squash and a few carrots that are not looking too tempting, turn them into a vegetable curry – just fry an onion and curry paste, add vegetables and simmer. Or, if you want something less spicy, add some stock and make a delicious soup.

Better still, before the vegetables get too sad and lose too many nutrients, freeze them. Prepare the vegetables as necessary then cook them in boiling water for 1–2 minutes (this kills off the spoiling enzymes), drain well, then plunge into cold water to stop the cooking process. Drain really well. If possible, freeze on baking sheets until firm (this way they don't stick together) then pack into freezer bags.

HERBS

Fresh herbs store better in the door of the fridge than the salad drawer. If you don't think you will use them all in the first few days after purchase, snip or chop and freeze them in ice-cube trays with a little water to add to dishes later.

Herbs can be expensive to buy in supermarkets, so why not grow your own in a windowbox or pot to give you a constant on-hand supply.

LEFTOVER RICE

Always keep any leftover rice in the fridge; never leave it in the pan overnight. Use leftover rice within 1 day or freeze it. Always reheat rice thoroughly as it can contain food-poisoning bacteria.

Leftover rice is ideal for a quick egg-fried rice supper. Fry a diced onion, add cooked rice and fry for 5 minutes until hot, then add cooked prawns and peas and fry for 2–3 minutes until hot. Add beaten eggs, stir until scrambled then flavour with soy sauce and sesame oil.

COOKED MEATS

• It's tempting to cook a larger roast than is needed so you can use the leftovers to make another meal. The reality is that those leftovers rarely get used unless you have planned what to do with them. The Food Standards Agency says that leftover meat should be stored in a cold fridge and eaten within 2 days. Place in the coldest part of the fridge, well wrapped to prevent drying out.

• The easiest way to use leftovers is to fry strips of beef or lamb with sliced onions and red or green peppers until tender and well heated through, then serve wrapped in flour tortillas with salsa, guacamole, soured cream, Greek yogurt or sweet chilli sauce. Or use meat in stir fries, curry, tagine or shepherd's pie.

• Leftover bolognese, casseroles and stews should be cooled as quickly as possible then kept chilled in the fridge for 2 days or frozen. Always reheat cooked meals thoroughly – the centre should reach boiling point and be cooked for 10 minutes to ensure it is safe to eat. Never reheat food more than once.

COOKED CHICKEN

• Leftover cooked chicken will keep for 2 days in a fridge. If you don't fancy using cold cooked chicken for salads, serve it in a hot supper. Boil chicken bones to make a quick stock to flavour a risotto and add the cooked chicken. Make an instant curry using curry paste, or fry cooked chicken with leeks, add some cream and serve with mash.

• Always reheat chicken thoroughly to ensure it is cooked right through to the centre.

A cost-conscious larder

Keep a stock of versatile ingredients in your storecupboard to help make inexpensive meals at a moment's notice.

- Rice shouldn't just be served on the side – use it to create paellas, rice salads and tasty one-pot dishes.

- Risotto rice makes a quick supper with any leftover chicken, prawns or veg.

- Couscous is an instant starchy base for suppers and salads.

- Pesto sauce adds flavour to pasta, chicken, mashed potato and fish dishes.

- Canned fish, such as tuna, mackerel, sardines and salmon, is useful for pasta dishes, salads and, of course, as sandwich fillers.

- A jar of roasted red peppers is ideal for adding to pasta, as extra topping on pizzas, and stews and casseroles for flavour.

- Curry paste is fantastic for making speedy curries. Mix a spoonful with Greek yogurt and paint on lamb or chicken for instant tandooris.

- Greek yogurt keeps well in the fridge and doesn't split when used in cooking, so stir into pan juices to make a creamy sauce, add to fish pies, use as a pasta sauce, add to curries, stir into mashed potato or whiz with red peppers or pesto to make an instant dip. It is also delicious in desserts. The 0% fat version is also thick and creamy, but because of the zero fat content this is not so stable when used in cooking.

- Half-empty jars of red peppers, pesto sauce and cook-in sauces will keep for a short while in the fridge – check the label, or freeze them in the jar or decanted into tiny freezer-proof containers. Buy a marker pen and label the lids of any food containers, or you'll never identify the contents in a few weeks' time.

Make friends with your freezer

Frozen foods are often excellent value, and as these foods are frozen as soon as they are picked or processed, they are often fresher than ready meals or prepared foods that you find in the chiller cabinet. Plus you only cook what you need when you need it, so there's less waste.

Freeze your leftovers but stick a list of what you've frozen on the freezer door – it's a great aide-mémoire when thinking about what to cook each night.

If you've bought in bulk because of a BOGOF offer, use the food by cooking larger quantites of a recipe – pasta sauces, stews, casseroles, soups – and freeze portions ready for those nights when you're too tired to cook from scratch.

Best-before and use-by dates

Don't be confused between best-before and use-by dates: best before indicates that the food is at its best before that date in terms of quality and taste, but it doesn't mean that it will be unsafe after that. You have a margin of 1 or 2 days to use the product after the specified date, but use your common sense. If a product looks or smells funny, chuck it.

Use-by dates, on the other hand, feature on foods that are likely to go off after a short period of time, and these may well be unsafe to eat after that date.

Index

Picture and recipe credits

Harper Collins would like to thank the following for providing photographs:

Steve Baxter pp10–11, p13, p17, p35, p47, p49, p51, p63, p65, p77, p81, p103, p105, p125, p131, p135, p153, p155, pp166–7, p169, p171, p173, p177, p179, p181; Lis Parsons p29, pp36–7, p41, p69, p87, p89, p91, p107, p145; Craig Robertson p15, p19, p25, p27, p33, p43, p55, p57, p59, p61, p67, p71, p73, p75, p83, p85, p93, p95, p97, p101, p109, p113, p115, p119, pp122–23, p127, p133, p139, p141, p143, p151, p159, p161, p163, p165, p175; Karen Thomas p21, p39, p111, pp146–7, p157; Stuart West p23, p45, p53, p79, pp98–99, p117, p129, p137, p149; Rob White p31

With thanks, too, for the following for creating the recipes for delicious. which are used in this book:

Kate Belcher p24, p30, p48, p72, p76, p154; Angela Boggiano p14, p42, p54, p56, p58, p60, p70, p92, p94, p96, p112, p126, p160, p162; Angela Boggiano and Alice Hart p132; Angela Boggiano and Kate Belcher p180; Matthew Drennan p174; Silvana Franco p74, p106, p138, p158, p164; Alice Hart p16, p18, p40, p66, p84, p86, p100, p118, p120, p150; Ghillie James p26, p32, p114, p176; Debbie Major p28, p68, p88, p134, p152; Lizzie Webb-Wilson p12, p20, p34, p38, p44, p46, p50, p62, p64, p78, p80, p82, p102, p104, p110, p124, p128, p130, p136, p140, p142, p148, p156, p168, p170, p172, p178, p180;
Lucy Williams p22, p52, p90, p116; Mitzie Wilson p144